THE LAWS OF THE

BOOK OF THE COVENANT

Introduction and commentary on
Exodus 20:22 to 23:19

Rev. Dr. R. D. Anderson

Copyright 2021

ISBN 978-0-6452484-3-2

Published by Pro Ecclesia Publishers
proecclesia.com.au

Preface

Already as a teenager the laws of the Book of the Covenant fascinated me. I would read and ponder what life must have been like in ancient Israel, at the same time asking myself what would happen if such laws were introduced into society today. It is therefore with satisfaction and thankfulness that, after the mature reflection of some 40 years, I am finally able to contribute a commentary on these laws. Needless to say, the congregation in Rockingham which I am currently privileged to serve, has enjoyed the first-fruits of these musings in a sermon series accompanied by a first-draft of the commentary for the benefit of the local bible clubs. I should also add that I have been greatly benefited by the questions and comments engendered by studying the Hebrew text along with its Greek translation together with Jayden Bosveld. Thanks Jayden!

The commentary has been laid out such that a reader with no knowledge of the biblical languages may profit from it. Following the introduction, my own translation of the text is provided together with the commentary on the law itself in regular type. The main commentary avoids the use of Hebrew or Greek in the main text. Hereafter each law is given in the original texts followed with a commentary on their language in smaller type. This can be ignored if the reader has no knowledge of the original languages.

The original text is given in both the Hebrew (following the Leningrad codex of AD 1008) and the Greek translation, known commonly as the Septuagint (or 'LXX') dating to the third century BC. Vocabulary aids are provided for the less common words and the Hebrew reader should also consult the relevant appendix to become familiar with classical Hebrew terminology regarding finances. The textual commentary often serves to justify aspects of the translation and may be used by those with knowledge of Hebrew and Greek. With respect to the Septuagint of this part of Exodus, Emmanuel Tov has cogently argued that the differences to the Massoretic text do indeed represent a slightly different Hebrew text which the translators used.

The Greek translator was quite literal, which is helpful in determining the Hebrew which he had in front of him. Although there are some additions to the text which may seem to be related to similar texts elsewhere in the Pentateuch (including texts within the same book), they are mostly translated in different ways which suggests that the translator is not himself engaging in harmonisations. The differences between the Massoretic text and that which the Greek translator used therefore need to weighed on their own merits. Reconstructions of the Hebrew *Vorlage* in the notes are usually pointed to aid the reader. The text of the Septuagint can often be verified by comparison with the Hebrew text of the Samaritan Pentateuch. While this text was updated and expanded by the Samaritans, and is thus of limited use in its own right, it does often serve to confirm textual variants found in the Septuagint. In my own translation, I have attempted – within reason – to remain quite literal, acknowledging that readers will have the ability to compare this translation with that from their own bibles. Names have therefore also been more literally transliterated from the Hebrew than is common in English bibles (e.g. Yisrael = Israel, Moshe = Moses). The divine name, often spelled 'Yahweh' in various publications, is here rendered both in my translation as well as in the text of the commentary with only a transliteration of the consonants 'YHWH'.

Quotations from other parts of Scripture are from the ESV unless otherwise marked. Versification is marked according to the English system except for the Hebrew and Greek texts, which vary by one verse throughout chapter 22.[1]

May the reader be profited from study of this part of God's holy Word and at the same time be reminded both of God's holiness and moral standards as well as his grace in providing legal provisions which take account of and deal with the various problems created by sin in society and personal life.

Rockingham, Western Australia
November 2021

---

1. The Göttingen edition of the Septuagint actually uses the same versification as English translations, but I have kept its numbering in line with the Hebrew for the sake of clarity.

Contents

INTRODUCTION 9
Legal courts. 12
Insufficient evidence requires an oath 13
A regulating set of principles. 17
The *Lex Talionis* 19
Substitution of retaliation for a fine 20
Accidental death 22
Conclusions. 23

COMMENTARY ON EXODUS 20:22 – 23:19
Worship of God. 27
Case Laws
   1. Slavery
      21:1-6 - Treatment of a Hebrew boy sold as slave. 37
      21:7-11 - Treatment of a Hebrew girl sold as slave-wife 48
Laws with penal sanctions
   2. Assault
      21:12-17 - Murder / manslaughter, parent-child crimes 57
      21:18-19 - Assault against a freeman 73
      21:20-21 - Assault against a slave 76
      21:22-25 - Unintentional assault on a pregnant woman
      and the lex talionis 80
      21:26-27 - Permanent damage to a slave by lashing out. 86
   3. Laws involving animals
      21:28-32 - Laws concerning a goring head of cattle. 90

21:33-34 - Death of another's animal in one's uncovered pit . . 99

21:35-36 - One's head of cattle kills another man's
head of cattle . . . .
. . . . 101

22:1-4 - Theft of animals. 105

22:5 - Accidental grazing of another's field 110

22:6 - Damage caused by out of control fire. 113

22:7-9 - Theft of inanimate property in one's keeping. 115

22:10-13 - Damage / theft to an animal in one's keeping . . . 121

22:14-15 - Damage to an animal borrowed or hired. 127

4. Other laws

22:16-17 - Defilement of a man's virgin daughter. 130

22:18 - Death penalty for a sorceress 137

22:19 - Death penalty for bestiality 140

The Ban

22:20-21 - The ban for sacrifice to other gods, but a
sojourner not to be oppressed 141

Laws without sanctions

22:22-24 - Don't afflict widows or orphans 147

22:25 - No interest on loans to the poor 150

22:26-27 - Cloak as pledge to be returned before sunset . . . 152

22:28 - Don't declare gods or a ruler to be cursed. 156

22:29-31 - Dedications to God: first-fruits, first-born
animals, Israelites 160

23:1-3 - Don't give false evidence, follow the majority
in evil or be partial in a dispute 167

23:4-5 - Help your enemy's animal in trouble. 171

23:6-9 - Don't pervert justice, take a bribe or oppress
a sojourner. 175

23:10-11 - Six years of sowing, one year of rest. 180

23:12 - Six days work, one day rest (for animals, slaves,
sojourners). 185

23:13 - No mention of other gods 187

23:14-17 - Three annual feasts. 189

23:18 - Don't offer blood with leaven nor leave fat until
morning 194

23:19a - First-fruits to be brought 198

23:19b - Don't boil a kid in its mother's milk 199

APPENDICES 201
The Effect of the Sin of the Golden Calf. 201

Finances in Hebrew. 206

BIBLIOGRAPHY 209

Abbreviations

DCH — *The Dictionary of Classical Hebrew*, ed. D. J. A. Clines, 8 vols (Sheffield: Sheffield Academic Press, 1993–2011).

HAL — *The Hebrew and Aramaic Lexicon of the Old Testament*, ed. L. Koehler & W. Baumgartner *et al.* (Leiden: E.J. Brill, 1994–2000).

LXX — The Septuagint (the Greek translation of the Pentateuch supposedly completed in Egypt in the third century BC by 70 Jewish priests) according to the edition *Septuaginta*, vol. II, 1 *Exodus*, ed. J. W. Wevers (Göttingen: Vandenhoeck & Ruprecht, 1991).

MT — The Masoretic Text (as represented by *codex Leningradensis*).

Sam. Pent. — The Samaritan Pentateuch according to the edition *Der hebräische Pentateuch der Samaritaner*, ed. A. F. von Gall (Giessen: Töpelmann, 1918).

INTRODUCTION[2]

The title "Book of the Covenant" is taken from Exodus 24:7. To understand this title we need to appreciate that a 'covenant' (*b^{e}rith*) in Hebrew is, strictly speaking, an oath which is sworn with some ceremony making contractual promises.[3]

In the ceremony that followed the production of this "Book of the Covenant" the people *en masse* agreed to abide by all the words of this book, nevertheless it was YHWH who was said to be "cutting the covenant" (i.e. swearing the oath), namely, to be their God. The "Book of the Covenant" is the condition by which the people remain in this relationship with God (cf. Gen. 18:18). Exodus 24:7-8 therefore reads as follows:

> *[7] Then he took the Book of the Covenant and read it in the hearing of the people. And they said, "All that the* LORD *has spoken we will do, and we will be obedient." [8] And Moses took the blood and threw it on the people and said, "Behold the blood of the covenant that the* LORD *has made* (lit. 'cut') *with you in accordance with all these words."*

The content of this scroll is referred to in verse three, "the words of the LORD and all the ordinances (*mišpātîm*)". These "words of the LORD" refer back to the revelation which Moses had received from God when he ascended the mountain for the first time, revelation we find in Exodus 20:22 – 23:33.[4]

---

2. An earlier version of this introduction has been published as: "The Book of the Covenant and Elders" in *The Eternal Word Speaks Today* (Wipf & Stock, 2010).
3. See Anderson[7].
4. I will not discuss various form critical theories of the make-up of the Book of the Covenant, its dating, and its place in the Book of Exodus. That is a subject apart (for summaries see, e.g. Houtman, 87-106 and Childs, 452-61). I accept its *prima facie* place in the canon as the revelation which God gave to Moses on the mountain.

The book itself is divided into three sections. It begins with a section on the worship of God. At 21:1 we have a title for the next section: "These are the *mišpāṭîm* (i.e. 'judgments')". There follows a lengthy section of judicial laws, beginning with a series of 'judgments' or case laws, which most appropriately fall under the rubric *'mišpāṭîm'*,[5] but also incorporating other kinds of legal formulations. The book concludes at 23:20-33 with an exhortation regarding the angel which will accompany the Israelites to the promised land.

The legal section itself is easily divided into two main sections. After the case laws on the sale of a son or daughter into slavery, the first main section (21:12 – 22:19) concerns judgments and laws to which penalties are attached.[6]

This is followed by a bridge (22:20-21) dealing with the ban and its consequences for the Israelites (see commentary). The second main section proper (22:22 – 23:19) concerns various laws and admonitions without penalties. This second section might, perhaps, appropriately be termed 'righteousness' (*tsᵉdhaqah*), although this feminine noun and its masculine cognate (*tsedheq*) are not actually used in the book of Exodus. Elsewhere in the Hebrew bible both 'judgment' (*mišpāṭ*) and 'righteousness' (*tsᵉdhaqah*) are used as a common pair (Gen. 18:19; Isa. 56:1; Ezek. 18:5, 19, 21, 27; 33:14, 16, 19; Ps. 106:3; Prov. 8:20; 16:8; 21:3). Strictly speaking 'righteousness' is more relational and concrete, taking into account circumstances, situation, and needs in a merciful and gracious way, which reflects God's own character. It is precisely this kind of 'righteousness', which is prescribed in the second section.

---

5. On *mišpāṭ*, see further Johnson, 86-98, esp. 94-95.
6. The laws with penal sanctions are mostly case laws with a formal introduction using the Hebrew *kî* (the only other laws in this book to use this introduction are 23:4 and 5). This form occurs 17 times in this section. There are also four exceptions 21:12, 15, 16 and 17. The occurrence of this form enables us to discern where the different laws are separated from each other in this section. Distinguishing the various laws from each other in the ensuing section (without penal sanctions) is more difficult and therefore open to different interpretations. For further distinguishing characteristics between the two legal sections see Houtman, 90-91.

The stele containing the law code of Hammurabi, ca. 1772 BC. It stands 225cm tall and is currently exhibited in the Louvre, Paris.

It is the legal section, which concerns us in this introduction. Many liberal scholars argue that the whole legal section must postdate the Sinai encounter with God, among other things, because the laws (e.g. concerning ownership of fields, or the festival calendar) presuppose a settled life in the promised land.[7]

It is, however, not difficult to imagine that God at the Sinai desired to give his people a law code, which would be useful in the settled condition of the promised land. More difficult, on the surface, is the nature of the laws themselves. As Hyatt has correctly observed, the laws seem to be "fragmentary and incomplete, not including by any means all that one would expect to find in a genuine law code".[8] The 'judgments' seem to be specific case studies with little or nothing to connect them. They give the appearance of arising from legal precedent, that is, specific cases that were decided in the past. And yet the biblical text asks us to understand that God gave *this legal code in this form* to Moses for the Israelites.

An appropriate way of understanding these judgments seems to me to entail an understanding of the presuppositions they embody. That the

---
7. For example, Childs, 458.
8. *Exodus*, 218.

laws imply settlement in the promised land is only a small part of this. They imply much more. I would suggest that the judgments imply a court system (we might think of the elders at the gate, or of local or itinerant judges, cf. Exod. 18:13-26; Deut. 16:18-20; 1 Sam. 7:15-17)[9] and certain basic principles of both judicial process and punishment of the guilty.

Legal courts

In the first place, we may consider the presupposition of legal courts. From Exodus 18:13-16 it is clear that Moses was functioning as a judge for disputes among the Israelites. We read in verse 16:

> ... *when they have a dispute, they come to me and I decide between one person and another, and I make them know the statutes of God and his laws.*

'Statutes' and 'laws' of God (cf. Gen. 26:5) were therefore already known upon which Moses could base his judgments, laws which unfortunately are unknown to us. That God chose the form of 'case' laws for his revelation on the Sinai further implies an existing court system. The case laws of the book of the covenant would therefore function to repeat and supplement what was already known of God's revelation in the area of justice.[10]

A court system is also implied by a specific use of the word *'elōhîm* ('God' / 'gods'). In Exodus 21:6 and again in 22:8 and 9 the word *'elōhîm* is used in a way which Jewish tradition as well as many

---

9. On judges and judicial process in Israel see further De Vaux, 150-63.
10. The striking resemblance of this law code with the *codex Hammurabi* (dating to approximately 1772 BC) as well as the many differences, both in length and in detail, support the idea that such codes of case law long predate the days of Moses. Genesis 26:5 presupposes that Abraham too had such a legal code given to him by God. The common elements between the book of the covenant and other ancient legal codes may, at least partly, be a result of God having given such a legal code to the early patriarchs, a code whose influence later infiltrated the various cultures which grew out of them. Relevant similarities and differences between the code of Hammurabi and the Book of the Covenant will be mentioned in the commentary.

modern scholars have taken to refer to judges.[11] This word, especially when coupled with a singular verb, is rendered as a singular, usually translated 'God'. The plural form of the noun may in such a case be considered a plural of majesty.[12] When coupled with a plural verb it is translated 'gods'. In 22:9 the verb-form coupled with '^{e}lōhîm is plural. The context, however, prevents a reference to (pagan) gods. Therefore many interpreters (correctly, in my opinion) refer here to the judges who are given a title of majesty.[13] The same use of '^{e}lōhîm to refer to judges can be found in Judges 5:8; 1 Samuel 2:25; Psalms 58:1;[14] 82:1, 6; and 138:1. That this interpretation is correct is all the more apparent by the fact that throughout the Book of the Covenant, the God of Israel is always referred to as 'Yhwh' or 'Yhwh our God' (outside of these passages, which surely refer to judges).[15]

Insufficient evidence requires an oath

In the second place, we should consider the fact that the need to determine sufficient evidence is presupposed. The question of (in)sufficient evidence is what lies behind the law in Exodus 22:10-11. When someone is given a domestic animal to look after and something happens to it (it dies, is hurt or is driven away), then the safekeeper is to swear on oath that he was not responsible for what happened. The implication is that the safekeeper in such a case is not required to make restitution to the owner. The owner is to be satisfied with the oath, for in the event that the safekeeper is lying Yhwh himself will avenge the misuse of his holy name (cf. Lev. 19:11-12[16]). It is evident

---

11. The Septuagint renders hā'^{e}lōhîm in Exod. 21:6 as "the court of God," cf. the Peshitta and Targums (Houtman, 122).

12. Kautzsch, § 124 g; *HAL* s.v. "'^{e}lōah and '^{e}lohim,*" B.1 and 2; Van der Merwe et al., 250 ("royal plural"); Waltke & O'Connor, 122-23 ("honorific plural").

13. There is in this case (with a plural verb) no justification for the rendering 'God' (contra e.g. Sarna). The NKJV translates 'judges', which is, of course, an interpretation of the more literal 'gods'.

14. I accept the common emendation of the Massoretic Text's 'ēlem ('silence') to 'ēlîm ('gods').

15. The word '^{e}lōhîm is used to refer to pagan gods and once to refer to accidental causes (21:13).

16. These two verses in Lev. 19 should be read together as one legal unit (legal

that the use of the oath is required because there is no further evidence available to actually prove what happened to the animal of the owner. Equally evident is the fact that the owner suspects that the safekeeper is not telling the whole truth. Otherwise he would not have appealed to the judges. It is just this use of the oath in cases of insufficient evidence, which the letter to the Hebrews refers to:

> *For people swear by something greater than themselves, and in all their disputes an oath is final for confirmation.* (Hebr. 6:16, cf. Deut. 6:13; 10:20)

Such an oath is generally known as an oath of purgation because the person taking the oath purges himself, by this procedure, from an aspersion of guilt. It is clear elsewhere in Scripture that such an oath of purgation was normally to take place in the temple before YHWH himself. We read in 1 Kings 8:31-32, a section from the prayer of Solomon at the dedication of the temple:

> *If a man sins against his neighbor and is made to take an oath and comes and swears his oath before your altar in this house, then hear in heaven and act and judge your servants, condemning the guilty by bringing his conduct on his own head, and vindicating the righteous by rewarding him according to his righteousness.* (cf. 2 Chron. 6:22-23)[17]

A specific example of such an oath is provided in Numbers 5:11-31 where a fairly elaborate ritual is used in the case of a husband who suspects his wife of adultery. The wife is brought to the temple and made to undergo an oath of purgation. Standing before the officiating priest with a special grain offering, she accepts a very specific self-

---

units in this part of the law are separated from each other by the concluding phrase "I am YHWH"). As such, false swearing is here directly related to court cases where there is a charge of theft or dealing falsely with one's neighbour.

17. Herein lies the background to Prov. 29:24 (literally translated), "Whoever is a partner with a thief hates his own life; he hears a curse, but reveals nothing". He hates his life because he is allowing God to curse him after he has been adjured to tell the truth.

imprecating curse with a double 'amen' and drinks a special curse-drink.[18]

Another specific ritual is recorded in Deuteronomy 21:1-9 for the case of an unsolved murder in the open country (where there is little likelihood of witnesses). The elders of the town nearest the victim must break a heifer's neck and wash the blood into a stream in an unfarmed valley. They must wash their hands over the heifer and swear, presumably on behalf of the town they represent, that they are not guilty of the murder nor did they witness it. It is unclear whether such rituals were typical of all oaths of purgation. It would seem that normally such oaths involved non-specific curses. In Exodus 22:10 the

---

18. This law does not, on the surface, seem very attractive. A husband who suspects his wife of adultery, even if he has no evidence, may bring her to the tabernacle and have her undergo this seemingly degrading ritual whereby she asks YHWH to curse her if she is not telling the truth. What is more, the wife has no right to make her husband undergo the same ritual. The most difficult verse is perhaps v.31 "The man shall be free from iniquity, but the woman shall bear her iniquity." It is clear that it cannot be the intention to say that men are allowed to commit adultery while women are not! If there was evidence for adultery, then both men and women had the right to appear before the elders at the gate to bring charges. The possible guilt of the man here, is the guilt of wrongly being jealous of his wife, accusing her of adultery when she had, in fact, been faithful. If, after completion of this ritual, it becomes clear that the woman is accepted by God, and thus not an adulteress, there is no punishment for the wrongful accusation of her husband. If the woman dared to come before YHWH when she was guilty (of adultery), then there is a certain punishment for her — not the death penalty, but physical punishment from God which results in the inability to bear any more children. This fact will have meant that in practice very few guilty women would have dared to undergo the ritual. This law will have been used for women who were wrongly accused by their husbands of unfaithfulness and came to YHWH for justification of their innocence. This law is therefore given to provide protection to a woman when she encounters the social dangers of a jealous husband. It does not tackle the problem of the sin of such jealousy itself. For this reason a wrongly jealous man is not punished (as an incentive for him to bring his wife to the tabernacle in such an eventuality). And that is why a woman equally jealous of her husband does not have the right to bring him to the tabernacle for such a ritual. The law concerns the protection of the socially weak in society. A jealous husband might terrorise his wife (for potential dangers see Exod. 21:10), but a jealous wife was not a danger to her husband in the same way. See further Anderson[1] and Anderson[3].

phrase "if he has not laid his hand on the property of his neighbour" (literal translation) uses an 'if' clause (*'im* / אִם), well-known in oath formulations. The apodosis (i.e. the 'then' clause) of such oaths was sometimes vaguely expressed, for example, "God do so to me and more also, if ..." (2 Sam. 3:35, cf. 1 Sam. 3:17), but moſt often not even expressed with so many words at all.[19]

The use of an oath in cases presenting insufficient evidence enables us to diagram the basic system of justice presupposed by the laws in the Book of the Covenant as follows:

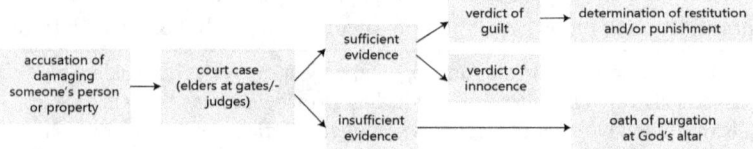

An accusation of one person against another inevitably involves damage to one's person or property (slander is not a criminal offence unless there is such damage).[20]

If the judges determine that there is insufficient evidence an oath of purgation is applied (cf. Hebr. 6:16). This means that the accused must take an oath that he has not harmed his neighbour (or his property) and asks God to punish him if he is lying. The matter is effectively given over into God's hands and the accuser is bound to leave the matter there and take no further action (unless, we may suppose, more evidence should come to light). If there is sufficient evidence for a trial, the judges will pronounce a verdict. We learn in Deuteronomy

---

19. See further *HAL, s.v.* " אִם " section 4.
20. An exception is made in the case of a curse againſt one's parents (Exod. 21:17, cf. Lev. 20:9). However, we should bear two things in mind respecting this law. Firſtly, that invoking a curse involves asking God (or gods) to injure one's parents. Secondly, that the verb קלל (*Piel*) involves treating a person with contempt and humiliation, an example of which is given in Deut. 21:18-21 (see Sarna, 123). It is intereſting to note that the prohibition in Exodus 22:28 againſt cursing judges (אֱלֹהִים , 'God' is probably not intended, for that would be a capital offence, cf. Lev. 24:11-15) or a ruler (נָשִׂיא) of the people is located in the second section of laws and therefore does not incur a penal sanction.

17:8-13 that cases too difficult for local courts could be handed over to a central court in the place where God had chosen to reside (which later became Jerusalem).

A regulating set of principles

A third, and perhaps most significant, presupposition which these laws embody is a regulating set of principles for the determination of punishment. Such principles are nowhere enunciated in the laws of Moses which have been handed down to us, but may be discerned by a study of these case laws. The case laws themselves are surely intended to provide examples of special circumstances and exceptions to these general governing principles.

We should remember that it is not the intention of the Book of the Covenant to be a completely new legal system for Israel. It is not a 'lawbook' in the modern sense of that word, wherein all possible situations and loopholes need to be covered. With these judgments God concerns himself with supplementing and correcting judicial practice and custom among the Israelites. We saw above that already before the Sinai encounter, Moses could speak of the statutes and laws which God had given for judging the people (Exod. 18:16).

The principles upon which punishment of any crime is determined may be summarised in a relatively simple way. All cases of damage may be placed into one of three categories as follows:

> *1) Damage inflicted with intent to harm requires restitution and the application of the* lex talionis *(eye for eye, etc.) to determine punishment*
>
> *2) Damage inflicted through negligence requires restitution*
>
> *3) Damage inflicted by accident does not require restitution*

The principle of restitution is one which permeates the jurisprudence here. Time and again the issue at stake is whether or not restitution should be granted. Medical expenses and compensation for lost work provide restitution for an injury (21:19). The owner of an uncovered pit is held responsible for domestic animals which fall into it and must make restitution (21:34). A thief must make restitution (22:3), one whose animal grazed another's field (22:5), one whose fire went out of control (22:6), one who borrowed another's animal and it became harmed (22:14). Many other case laws, which do not mention restitution specifically may also be interpreted in this light. For example, a father, who is responsible for guarding his daughter's virginity, is recompensed with the proceeds of a stiff fine when his daughter's virginity is taken by another male (22:16-17), rendering her potentially unmarriable.

The case laws show clearly that restitution is generally not required when the damage is caused by accident. An animal given in safekeeping that dies or is hurt or driven away does not require restitution unless it can be proven that the damage was caused by the safekeeper himself (22:10-11). It is likewise implied that inanimate property, which is damaged when given in safekeeping, does not have to be restored. The law in 22:7-8 is only interested in whether or not the safekeeper himself laid his hands on the property. Other case laws provide nuances and exceptions to this general rule of thumb. When a person has borrowed an animal to use for himself, he remains responsible for it and must provide restitution even if it is hurt by accident (22:14). However, the responsibility remains with the owner if he was with the animal at the time (22:15). Another special case concerns a head of cattle, not known as dangerous, which gores someone else to death. The owner of the animal is not held responsible for the accident, but the dangerous animal must be killed (21:28).

The last example touches on a series of special cases involving the death of someone. A dead person cannot be restored to the family. It would appear that any thought of *restitution* by monetary recompense is excluded. The sanctions involved when a death has occurred should be viewed as punishment and not a form of restitution. Before we return to this point, however, it is necessary to discuss the general principle for punishment (retribution), which governs the case laws, namely, the *lex talionis*.

The Lex Talionis

The principle is expressed in 21:23-25, "life for life, eye for eye, tooth for tooth," etc. A simple example of the application of this principle is the punishment normally accorded a thief. He is to pay double what he stole (22:4, 7, 9), that is, restitution and a retribution equivalent to the amount he stole.[21]

When applied to physical injuries, there is good reason to believe that the principle was generally only literally applied in the case of death. The principle "eye for eye, tooth for tooth" was a legal principle stating the need for a punishment equal to the crime. This principle is found in two other places in God's law, Leviticus 24:17-20 and Deuteronomy 19:21. Essentially it provides that each sinful deed must receive an equally fitting punishment. In each case it is a principle with a judicial context. For this reason the Lord Jesus turned so sharply against the Pharisees when they abused this principle as an excuse to justify personal revenge (Matt. 5:38-39).[22]

---

21. The case laws make an exception to this principle only in the case of stolen cattle or sheep/goats which are not recovered.

22. In the sermon on the Mount Jesus was not occupying himself with writing a new law. His intention was to maintain God's moral law in all its details (Matt. 5:17-19 – ceremonial laws are nowhere addressed in his sermon). In doing this he had a clear desire to reach further than the outward literal text into the 'righteousness' (צְדָקָה) of the matter (Matt. 5:20). At this period the Hebrew term 'righteousness' (צְדָקָה) had acquired the sense of a righteousness that takes account of the circumstances and situation of the person in trouble and acts mercifully. Applied to the poor this often implied almsgiving, applied to courtroom situations it implied mediation instead of strict judgement. Jesus makes further application to the heart and thoughts of the person concerned. In Matthew 5 Jesus goes through several commandments and drives their message home into the heart in a hyperbolic fashion (i.e. with intentional exaggeration). In doing this he sets himself against the Rabbinical traditions of his time. A couple of examples should suffice: In v.27 he speaks about adultery. Jesus drives this home when he hyperbolically proposes that if one's right eye causes him to sin, he should pluck it out. Even though it is true that it would be better for a person to lose one of his body parts than to have his whole body thrown into hell, it is not Jesus' intention to say that one should literally pluck out his eyes. If that were the case everyone would need to blind themselves. Jesus speaks in hyperbole, but his point is thereby all the more forcefully made. He reaches

This principle of a just retaliation means that when a victim loses a body part, he may demand (before the judges) that the perpetrator's same body part be removed as punishment. If your neighbour plucks out your right eye, then, according to God's law, you may demand from the judge that his right eye also be removed. This is not restitution, it is retribution. The practice may sound somewhat cruel, but we should understand that in reality it seldom appears to have been carried out literally. The fact that the victim *may* demand the perpetrator's body part gives him bargaining leverage for the *alternative* of allowing the literal vengeance to be commuted into a fine (cf. Josephus, *Ant.* 4.280). In other words, instead of demanding the right eye of the perpetrator, the victim may demand a financial penalty. The victim will of course benefit much more from a fine (which he receives — not the court) than the right eye of the perpetrator. Because it is the victim who gives permission for substitution and who has the right to negotiate the extent of the fine, there is not so much scope for discrimination between rich and poor. If the perpetrator was wealthy, more money could be extracted from him in lieu of a body part, than from a poor man.

Substitution of retaliation for a fine

Although there is no direct legal text in the selection of Mosaic law handed down to us which outlines the substitution of physical retaliation with a monetary fine, there are several examples of this practice. The law in Exodus 21:29-30 provides for commuting a death penalty into

---

into the heart when he states that even looking at a woman lustfully amounts to adultery. This is hyperbole (exaggeration) in the sense that whilst lusting after a woman is adultery in God's eyes, it has no civil consequences (the court does not punish sins of the heart, and therefore, for example, lusting after a woman cannot be considered a valid ground for divorce). In v.33 Jesus speaks about breaking one's oath. He speaks hyperbolically when he states that one should not make any oath at all (at the same time criticising the Jewish practice of swearing by the name of things instead of by the name of God). But Jesus himself was later to accept an oath (Matt. 26:63-64, cf. Gal. 1:20; Hebr. 6:13-18 and LD 37 of the Heidelberg Catechism). Jesus reaches into the heart when he states that one's yes should be yes, and one's no, no. The same principle of interpretation must be applied to what Jesus says concerning the *lex talionis*.

a fine. From the book of Proverbs we learn that the same possibility of substitution existed for adultery. The prescribed punishment for adultery is the death penalty (Lev. 20:10; Deut. 22:22).[23] However Proverbs 6:32-35 (cf. 13:7-8) warns us that the plaintiff (the injured marriage partner) in an adultery case could become so angry that he would not even be prepared to consider a fine as substitute for the death penalty. We see here that the right to insist on having the official sentence executed remains with the plaintiff.[24]

> *He who commits adultery lacks sense; he who does it destroys himself. ... For jealousy makes a man furious, and he will not spare when he takes revenge* (lit. "in the day of vengeance [i.e. at court]"). *He will accept no compensation; he will refuse though you multiply gifts.* [i.e. even if you offer him a fortune as redemption].

That such substitution was standard legal practice is quite clear from the one case where God forbids it. We read in Numbers 35:31-33:

> *Moreover, you shall accept no ransom for the life of a murderer, who is guilty of death, but he shall be put to death. And you shall accept no ransom for him who has fled to his city of refuge, that he may return to dwell in the land before the death of the high priest. You shall not pollute the land in which you live, for blood pollutes*

---

23. Note that, although the penalty in a passage such as Lev. 20:10 is often translated as "shall surely be put to death", this is not a necessary translation. The Hebrew use of the infinitive absolute as an internal accusative does add emphasis, but the finite verb does not necessarily have to be understood as indicative. The context is determinative (see discussion in Jouön/Muraoka §123d-p). The phrase מוֹת־יוּמָת may therefore be translated as "he may surely be killed" or "he should surely be killed" (a translation which still leaves the possibility open for an unexpressed conditional clause "unless his death is ransomed"). The use of the internal accusative serves to emphasis the maximum penalty here.

24. This also helps us to understand Joseph's initial reaction to the pregnancy of Mary. He was well within his rights to choose not to press for the death penalty, but to quietly arrange for a divorce instead (Matt. 1:19). Given that Matthew emphasises that Joseph was 'righteous', we should understand the concept of 'righteousness' here in terms of that outlined in footnote 22, namely, a righteousness that takes account of the circumstances and situation of the person in trouble and acts mercifully.

> the land, and no atonement can be made for the land for the blood that is shed in it, except by the blood of the one who shed it.

The penalty for murder or manslaughter may not be commuted into a fine, implying that for most other penalties this was an acceptable solution.

At this point, we can return to the question of sanctions when a death has occurred. As stated above, this is always a special case in view of the fact that restitution is impossible. Exodus 21:12-14 (cf. Num. 35) makes it clear that when death is the result of an action which was designed to harm the person, the death penalty applies according to the principle of *talio*. However, Numbers 35, as cited above, rules that in this case the punishment was mandatory and not able to be substituted for a fine. The same text also states the reason for this measure, namely that blood pollutes the land and demands an atonement by blood. The wording here recalls Genesis 9:6 where the death penalty is also required for murder. In Genesis 9 one other important facet is added, namely that man is created in the image of God. The honour of God himself is assaulted when a person is killed. His image is destroyed.

Accidental death

When death is the result of an accident caused not by the person himself, but some aspect of his property, the law separates two distinct cases. The first instance is that when death is a result of negligence by the owner, as in the case of an unprotected dangerous head of cattle (cf. Deut. 22:8). The governing principles for punishment would demand restitution, but no punishment. However, in this case restitution is not possible. Therefore the owner is made liable to the death penalty, but in this instance it is commutable (Exod. 21:29-30).

The second instance is death by accident without negligence. Here the law isolates two possibilities. If the death is an accident caused by the property of the owner (e.g. a head of cattle which unexpectedly gores someone to death) there is no penalty (21:28).

However, when accidental death (with or without a degree of negligence) is caused by the person himself, he is compelled to flee to a city of refuge until the death of the high priest (Num. 35:9-11). Such provision of sanctuary is presupposed in Exodus 21:14 when it is stated that one who commits murder (death caused after intent to harm) may be removed from the sanctuary of the altar.

Conclusions

When we further reflect upon the basic principles of punishment in the Book of the Covenant and the way in which the case laws apply them to difficult circumstances, at least two things may strike us. In the first place, we nowhere find provisions for the cutting off of hands or other body parts as pure punishment (e.g. for theft) as many of the other Ancient Near Eastern legal codes require. In the second place, there is no provision for confinement as a judicial sanction. In fact, the whole principle of rehabilitation, if it was considered a principle at all, remains secondary.[25]

Judicial process seeks primarily to provide restitution and an appropriate retribution. The retribution in most cases serves to benefit the victim and satisfy his upright demand that the wrong perpetrated against him be avenged. In this way, the punishments are designed to promote harmony and peaceful relations in society.

There is much to be learned here by elders of the church, especially when their task of promoting the peace in the congregation is taken seriously. They are given a ruling function in Christ's congregations (cf. Acts 20:28; Hebr. 13:17) and may be expected to function as judges in cases of civil disputes (1 Cor. 6:1-11). In that respect the Book of the Covenant, while not in every respect able to be applied today, does provide basic principles of justice from which we may learn. They are principles given to us by the revelation of our God, the same God, who provides reconciliation with himself through the substitutionary punishment of his own Son, Jesus Christ.

---

25. Rehabilitation may be considered to be effected through observance of the principle of restitution, but this idea is not made specific in the law.

COMMENTARY ON EXODUS 20:22 – 23:19

20:22-26

WORSHIP OF GOD

Translation

(address to the whole assembly)

²² And Y<small>HWH</small> said to Moshe, 'Thus you shall say to the sons of Yisrael: You have seen that I spoke (the 10 commandments) with you from heaven.

²³ You shall not make gods of silver next to me nor shall you make gods of gold for yourselves.

(address to individuals)

²⁴ You shall make for me an altar of earth and on it you shall sacrifice your whole-burnt offerings and your peace offerings, your flock and your herd in every place where I cause my name to be remembered and I will come to you and I will bless you.

²⁵ And if you make for me an altar of stones, you shall not build with dressed stones. When you have brandished your chisel on them, then you have profaned them.

²⁶ And you shall not ascend my altar on steps so that there is no revealing of your nakedness upon it.

Commentary

God's speaking requires an answer

These verses must be seen in the context of God's awesome speaking of the 10 commandments at Mt. Sinai.²⁶

---

26. The point being made here is not that God speaks (regardless of content)

The people had become so afraid that they had asked Moses to ascend the mountain and receive the rest of the Law on their behalf. When Moses returned, the first thing that Yhwh wished to reveal to his people was the correct way to approach him.

It is to be noted that here (and in Deut. 4:36) God is said to have spoken, not from the mountain, but from the heavens. Throughout Deuteronomy four and five Moses also stresses that God spoke from the midst of the fire (that is, the lightning, cf. Deut. 4:12, 15, 33; 5:4, 22, 24, 26). In fact it is never stated that God spoke from the mountain. Exodus 19:20 does, however, state that God came down to the top of the mountain in order to speak privately with Moses there.

What follows may be considered to be directly related to God's speaking. As with the patriarchs, when God spoke or appeared to them, they were expected to answer in prayer. Prayer could only be prepared for with a gift, usually a sacrifice, which in turn required the construction of an altar. The laws that follow have to do with the necessary preparations for such prayer, whether that be the required absence of any other god, or the kind of altar to be used. It should be remembered that it is highly unlikely that Israel would have actually sacrificed (or per consequence, prayed) during the sojourn in Egypt. God did not reveal himself and speak to the people during this time. When God appeared to Moses at the burning bush (Exod. 3), he needed to introduce himself. When Moses and Aaron told the Pharaoh that his slaves, the Hebrews, needed to leave Egypt, this was so that they could sacrifice to "the God of the Hebrews" (Exod. 5:1-3). Obviously this was something that had not been possible to do in Egypt or Pharaoh would have had an easy answer. The situation reveals something of the immense change in circumstances which God's calling of his people to himself through Moses brought about. The first recorded sacrifice from this period was performed at Rephidim after God enabled the Amalekites to be defeated and again spoke to Moses (Exod. 17:8-15). It is clear that the Israelites had priests (Exod. 19:22), who were

---

from heaven, but that in this concrete instance they have heard God speaking certain statements (the 10 commandments) from heaven. See my textual note on the *Piel* of דבר. In this respect both the NKJV and ESV are misleading.

probably consecrated first-born sons.[27]

All this provides the context for the opening laws of the book of the covenant.

No idols next to YHWH

Two separate, but related, laws are given. The first is addressed to the Israelites corporately (plural verbs and pronouns are used).

An altar of uncut stone from Tel Arad in Israel, ca. 950 BC (Photo: Madain Project)

They must not make images of gods to be next to God in his place of worship. From everything that the Israelites would have seen and known from Egypt (and throughout the ancient world), it would have seemed completely normal to them to fashion idols of other gods to keep their God company. Even if they acknowledged that YHWH himself could not be sculptured, there would have been a significant temptation to decorate his place of worship with other cult statues. We know from Joshua 24:14 that many Israelites served other gods in Egypt alongside the God of their forefather Abraham and so the temptation to worship idols will have been strong, particularly when the God of their forefathers seemed so fearful and distant (not allowing images of himself). This first law forbidding idols may presuppose some kind of permanent place for worshipping God, where corporate worship could be held.

The law of the altar

The ensuing law of the altar is addressed to the individual Israelite and seems to presuppose personal or family worship. The law concerns the altars to be used in approaching God. It becomes clear that the initiative for such an ability to speak to God always comes from God

---

27. See the appendix on the effect of the sin with the golden calf.

himself. Only in those places where he has previously caused his name to be remembered may an altar be built. In addition, an altar is not to be constructed in such a way that human artistry is evident. The situation envisaged is the need to worship and speak to Yhwh in a place where there is no established sanctuary. The worshipper must therefore construct a make-shift altar for this purpose. This law of the altar has engendered much scholarly discussion. It is not the place here to discuss various alternative explanations critical of Scripture, suffice to say that in the 19th century Wellhausen contrasted this law with the law in Deuteronomy 12 requiring sacrifice at a central sanctuary. He used it as evidence for the 'evolution' of Israel's religion. This older law, according to Wellhausen, allowed the Israelites to sacrifice upon a multitude of altars. It shows that the high places were perfectly legitimate. Later, in the time of Josiah, the book of Deuteronomy – again, according to Wellhausen – was fabricated with the law of Deuteronomy 12 stating that sacrifice is only legitimate in the central sanctuary. A major problem with Wellhausen's reconstruction is that this law cannot be interpreted to be in contradiction with the notion of a permanent sanctuary, for a permanent sanctuary is presupposed in the very same Book of the Covenant (cf. 23:17 and 19).[28]

What then is this law referring to? In the first place the law refers to altars which are built at places where Yhwh himself causes his name to be remembered. These are *not* private altars, built only on the whim of the worshipper. Nor does the law necessarily argue for a multiplicity of altars at the same time. At any time, when Yhwh causes his name to

---

28. Van Dam has argued that although high places were condemned in Num. 33:52, they seem to have been tolerated for a time, cf. 1 Sam. 9:11-24; 10:5-6; 1 Kgs. 3:4. He connects this toleration of high places with the removal of the ark of the covenant from the sanctuary in the time of Eli (1 Sam. 4). It is clear from Psalm 78 that this was God's judgment on the apostasy of Ephraim in whose territory the sanctuary resided at the time (i.e. in Shiloh). The ark remained separate from the tent of meeting until the construction of the temple under the reign of Solomon. It was only after the reunification of the sanctuary and the ark that the high places were once again mentioned with disapproval, e.g. 1 Kgs. 11:7. This suggests that the removal of the ark (i.e. the "glory of Israel," God's presence) also implied that there was no central sanctuary anymore. The concept of a central sanctuary was inextricably bound up with God's special presence there, symbolised in the ark of the covenant.

be remembered in a particular place, an altar may be built to worship him. The law looks back to the time of the patriarchs and the altars they built at special places where God was leading them, for example, Shechem (Gen. 12:6-7), Moriah (Gen. 22:2), Beersheba (Gen. 26:23-25), and Bethel (Gen. 35:1, cf. 12:8). After the Exodus an altar was built in this tradition at Rephidim by Moses, after God spoke to him (Exod. 17:8, 15). The law here gives regulations on how such altars ought to be built in the future (see e.g. Deut. 27:5-7; Josh. 8:30-31; Jud. 6:25-27).[29]

The sacrifices mentioned here (burnt and peace offerings) were the two basic parts of the normal sacrificial ritual, which therefore involved a minimum of two animals (one as a burnt offering and the other as a peace offering). The sin and guilt offerings mentioned in Leviticus were given for special cases. We probably ought to understand that together with the burnt offering belonged the grain offering, the libation of wine, the addition of salt and so forth. The peace offering was shared with God in that only the fat and the kidneys of that animal were presented on the altar.

After the slaughter of the animals, the blood was first splashed against the altar. As explained in Leviticus 17:11, the blood was viewed as the symbol of life and was given by God upon the altar to make atonement for the worshipper(s) (cf. Hebr. 9:22; Rom. 3:25). In this way, every sacrifice began with an atonement ritual. Only after the blood ritual for atonement had been dealt with, were the animals skinned and all the various ingredients placed or tied together on the altar. The sacrifice was then set alight and burned as a symbolic meal for YHWH (cf. Lev. 3:11; Ps. 50). The meat of the peace offering was eaten by those bringing the offering as a sacrificial meal. This law shows that the basic sacrificial procedure outlined in the laws of Moses also existed before the lawgiving at Sinai. The sacrifices mentioned here

---

29. The text does not specify what an 'altar of earth' would be made of. Suggestions have ranged from soil (which would make for a very temporary altar), mud bricks (although this could more simply have been stipulated by the term לְבֵנָה), or even just a 'natural altar' (cf. 2 Chron. 26:10). For discussion of these suggestions, see Sprinkle, 41-42.

are clearly expected to be already well-known to the Israelites. They probably go back to the patriarchs if not further.

Yhwh promises to come and bless the people when they sacrifice to him at the place in which he causes his name to be remembered. Sacrifice, of course, enables communion with Yhwh by speaking to him in prayer (prayer was usually accompanied by sacrifice). We learn from Leviticus 9:22-24 that the priests came out and pronounced God's blessing upon the people after the blood rites were completed and before the offerings were put to the flame. The blessing therefore signifies reconciliation with God through forgiveness of sins. This in turn means that one may expect God to be his protector and shepherd (i.e. heavenly king) in life.

The Design

The altar is to have no steps. It is interesting to note that the altar in the vision of Ezekiel (43:17) has steps on the East side. It has been suggested that the altar of burnt offerings for Solomon's temple must have had steps due to its great height (it was four times the size of the altar in the tabernacle, cf. 2 Chron. 4:1).[30] But this regulation does not concern the design of the altar in the tabernacle or temple. Rather, as noted above, it concerns memorial altars in special places where Yhwh causes his name to be remembered.

Furthermore, the altar of the tabernacle was designed after the sin of the golden calf and the consequent appointment of Levitical priests instead of the service of (first-born) sons (cf. 24:5 for offerings brought *before* the sin of the golden calf).[31] That this fact may be relevant is clear from the reason given in verse 26 for the prohibition on steps. The law presupposes that the pre-Aaronic priest (cf. Exod. 19:22-24) would be wearing some kind of simple linen loincloth which upon the ascent of stairs would expose one's genitals (cf. 2 Sam. 6:14, 20). The priestly clothing later specified for Aaron and his sons would not have engendered this problem (cf. Exod. 28:42-43). We might recall that a

---

30. It is unlikely that Lev. 9:22 indicates that the altar in the tabernacle had steps. It would seem that Aaron stood on top of the altar to give the blessing.
31. See the appendix on the effect of the sin of the golden calf.

discharge of semen or blood from the genitals made one unclean and thus temporarily debarred a person from worshipping God.[32] Pagan worship at this time often included cult prostitution. God's law makes such a practice impossible.

Text

[22] Εἶπεν δὲ κύριος πρὸς Μωυσῆν Τάδε ἐρεῖς τῷ οἴκῳ Ιακωβ καὶ ἀναγγελεῖς τοῖς υἱοῖς Ισραήλ Ὑμεῖς ἑωράκατε ὅτι ἐκ τοῦ οὐρανοῦ λελάληκα πρὸς ὑμᾶς· [23] οὐ ποιήσετε ἑαυτοῖς θεοὺς ἀργυροῦς, καὶ θεοὺς χρυσοῦς οὐ ποιήσετε ὑμῖν αὐτοῖς. [24] θυσιαστήριον ἐκ γῆς ποιήσετέ μοι καὶ θύσετε ἐπ' αὐτοῦ τὰ ὁλοκαυτώματα καὶ τὰ σωτήρια ὑμῶν, τὰ πρόβατα καὶ τοὺς μόσχους ὑμῶν ἐν παντὶ τόπῳ, οὗ ἐὰν ἐπονομάσω τὸ ὄνομά μου ἐκεῖ, καὶ ἥξω πρὸς σὲ καὶ εὐλογήσω σε. [25] ἐὰν δὲ θυσιαστήριον ἐκ λίθων ποιῇς μοι, οὐκ οἰκοδομήσεις αὐτοὺς τμητούς· τὸ γὰρ ἐγχειρίδιον ἐπιβέβληκας ἐπ' αὐτό, καὶ μεμίανται. [26] οὐκ ἀναβήσῃ ἐν ἀναβαθμίσιν ἐπὶ τὸ θυσιαστήριόν μου, ὅπως ἂν μὴ ἀποκαλύψῃς τὴν ἀσχημοσύνην σου ἐπ' αὐτοῦ.	וַיֹּאמֶר יְהוָה אֶל־מֹשֶׁה כֹּה תֹאמַר אֶל־בְּנֵי יִשְׂרָאֵל אַתֶּם רְאִיתֶם כִּי מִן־הַשָּׁמַיִם דִּבַּרְתִּי עִמָּכֶם: [23] לֹא תַעֲשׂוּן אִתִּי אֱלֹהֵי כֶסֶף וֵאלֹהֵי זָהָב לֹא תַעֲשׂוּ לָכֶם: [24] מִזְבַּח אֲדָמָה תַּעֲשֶׂה־לִּי וְזָבַחְתָּ עָלָיו אֶת־עֹלֹתֶיךָ וְאֶת־שְׁלָמֶיךָ אֶת־צֹאנְךָ וְאֶת־בְּקָרֶךָ בְּכָל־הַמָּקוֹם אֲשֶׁר אַזְכִּיר אֶת־שְׁמִי אָבוֹא אֵלֶיךָ וּבֵרַכְתִּיךָ: [25] וְאִם־מִזְבַּח אֲבָנִים תַּעֲשֶׂה־לִּי לֹא־תִבְנֶה אֶתְהֶן גָּזִית כִּי חַרְבְּךָ הֵנַפְתָּ עָלֶיהָ וַתְּחַלְלֶהָ: [26] וְלֹא־תַעֲלֶה בְמַעֲלֹת עַל־מִזְבְּחִי אֲשֶׁר לֹא־תִגָּלֶה עֶרְוָתְךָ עָלָיו:

---

32. See Anderson[4], §1.4A.

| גָּזִית, dressed stone | עֶרְוָה, nakedness |
| נוּף Hiph. to move to and fro (brandish) | |

20:22

כֹּה תֹאמַר אֶל־בְּנֵי יִשְׂרָאֵל / Τάδε ἐρεῖς τῷ οἴκῳ Ιακὼβ καὶ ἀναγγελεῖς τοῖς υἱοῖς Ισραήλ

The addition comes from Exod. 19:3, which reads: כֹּה תֹאמַר לְבֵית יַעֲקֹב וְתַגֵּיד לִבְנֵי יִשְׂרָאֵל.

כִּי מִן־הַשָּׁמַיִם דִּבַּרְתִּי עִמָּכֶם

Note that the *Piel* of דבר suggests the speaking of concrete words or defined statements. Speaking as such (without reference to content) requires the *Qal*. The point being made here is not that God speaks (regardless of content) from heaven, but that in this concrete instance they have heard God speaking certain statements (the 10 commandments) from heaven. See Jenni[2], 164-70; Anderson[8], 7.

20:23

תַעֲשׂוּן

The *paragogic nun* found with imperfect forms ending in ו is an archaism. It is regular in the spelling of cognate languages such as Ugaritic, Arabic and Aramaic. It is rare in late Biblical Hebrew or early rabbinic Hebrew, see further Joüon/Muraoka §44e.

אִתִּי / ἑαυτοῖς

Sprinkle[33] argues for the interpretation 'with me' in the sense of 'in my case'. He then goes on to understand 'gods of silver and gods of gold' in the sense of silver or gold images of YHWH. As far as I am aware, however, such a sense for אֵת ('with') is unattested elsewhere, while the sense 'with' = 'next to / besides' is normal for this word. The LXX is a little odd, given that a reflexive pronoun is appropriately used at the beginning of the sentence, but an awkward combination at the end. However it should be realised that there is considerable textual variation in the manuscripts. The LXX may have read תַּעֲשׂוּ לָכֶם for תַעֲשׂוּן אִתִּי.

---

33. Sprinkle, 35.

20:24

תַּעֲשֶׂה־לִּי / ποιήσετέ μοι

Unlike the law against other cult statues, the law of the altar is addressed in the singular, implying individual worship. The LXX keeps v.24a in the plural, changing to the singular from v.24b. Note the *daghesh forte conjunctivum* in the ל here and in v.25, which is used under certain circumstances when two words are brought close together, see further Jouön/Muraoka §18h-j.

אֲשֶׁר אַזְכִּיר אֶת־שְׁמִי אָבוֹא / οὗ ἐὰν ἐπονομάσω τὸ ὄνομά μου ἐκεῖ, καὶ ἥξω

In late Greek ἐάν is often used for ἄν. The LXX normally uses the verb ἐπονομάζω to translate קרא. Its use here may merely be a reflection of the more common idiom of 'naming a name' than any supposed alternate *Vorlage*. The LXX (cf. Sam. Pent. שמי שמה) also presupposes the (in Greek) redundant שם as well as a following ו, which were probably part of the Hebrew text. They may have been lost by haplography (from שמי שם ו). The MT punctuation, however, assumes the MT consonantal text, creating a pause after 'your cattle', which is necessary if there is no conjunction after 'in every place where I cause my name to be remembered'.

20:25

לֹא־תִבְנֶה אֶתְהֶן גָּזִית / οὐκ οἰκοδομήσεις αὐτοὺς τμητούς

The feminine pronoun as direct object refers back to the stones (אֲבָנִים), which, despite the masculine plural ending, is actually a feminine noun. The verb בנה can take two accusative objects, one of that which is built, and an accusative of respect referring to the material. Greek, however, does not normally add an accusative of material to the verb οἰκοδομέω. One might have expected ἐκ τμητῶν (λίθων). Wevers, however, points to parallels of this usage in LXX Deut. 27:6 and 3 Kgdm 18:32.

חַרְבְּךָ / τὸ ἐγχειρίδιον

The noun חֶרֶב is used for any short-bladed instrument, here a chisel. Note the omission of אֶת־, which is common when the direct object precedes the verb. Many LXX mss add the suffix σου.

עָלֶיהָ / ἐπ' αὐτό

The MT is referring to the stones, not the altar (which is masculine in Hebrew). The singular suffix in the Hebrew is a little odd, following upon אֶתְהֶן. We might have expected עֲלֵיהֶן, which appears to be what the LXX read. The LXX probably represents the correct text here (עֲלֵיהֶן ו for ו עָלֶיהָ, cf. Sam. Pent. ועליו), another example of haplography in the MT.

הֲנֻפְתָּ

Note this form without the helping vowel (which would otherwise have been הֲנִיפוֹתָ), cf. Davidson §30.5.

ו ׃ וַתְּחַלְלֶהָ / μεμίανται

The LXX presupposes a *Pual* 3rd person pl. imperfect (וַיְחֻלְלוּ), but the *Pual* of this verb is rare and then only found in the participle. The lack of καί at the beginning of v.26 is probably also involved in this variant (and certainly incorrect) reading of the Hebrew *Vorlage*. However, this suggests that the original reading may have had a plural suffix (וַתְּחַלְלֻן), cf. Sam. Pent., which has a 3rd pers. sing. masc. suffix: ותחללהו.

20:26

אֲשֶׁר לֹא־תִגָּלֶה / ὅπως ἂν μὴ ἀποκαλύψῃς

The use of אֲשֶׁר in a final sense is rare. We should have expected לְמַעַן, cf. Jouön/Muraoka §168f. The LXX possibly interprets the *Niphal* תִגָּלֶה as *Piel* תְגַלֶּה. But it is also possible that the LXX interpreted the *Niphal* as indicating the middle voice in an active sense.

21:1-6

CASE LAWS

1. SLAVERY

Treatment of a Hebrew boy sold as slave

Translation

¹ And these are the judgments which you shall set before them.

² When you acquire a Hebrew slave, he may serve you six years, but in the seventh he shall go out as a free man without payment.

³ If he comes alone, then he shall go out alone, if he is the husband[34] of a wife then his wife shall go out with him.

⁴ If his master gives him a wife and she bears him sons or daughters, the wife – and her children – shall belong to his master, while he goes out alone.

⁵ And if the slave plainly says, 'I love my master, my wife, and my sons, I will not go out a free man,

⁶ then his master shall bring him to the gods[35] and he shall bring him to the doorway or to the doorpost, and his master shall pierce his ear through with an awl and he shall serve him permanently.

---

34. The Hebrew word for 'husband' literally means 'master', although it is a different word to 'master' in the sense of owner (e.g. the master/owner of a slave).
35. I.e. 'judges' or perhaps 'God'. See the commentary.

Commentary

This law discusses the term and manumission procedure for a Hebrew boy sold as slave. The law characterises him as of marriageable age. In contrast to the slave law of Deuteronomy (see below) he is not presumed to hold title to any inherited land. Therefore, upon ending his period of slavery, it would be expected that he return to the family farm.

Debt slavery limited in duration and sex

Hebrew slaves were not to be permanent (unless of their own free will – see below). Upon a maximum of six years slavery the young man is to be set free. The owner was not to require the slave to purchase his freedom after the sixth year of service. He was to be set free without payment (i.e. payment by the slave). If he had been married upon entry into slave-service his wife (and, by implication, any children) were not to be withheld. They were not technically property of the master.[36] The master was, therefore, not to attempt by such means to compel the slave to remain in his service. Only if the wife of the slave had been *given* to him by the master, might he require her and her children to remain. The wife was then an independent slave of the master who had been paid for.[37]

Hebrews could sell themselves – or more regularly (see below) their sons – into slavery when there was no possibility of paying off a debt.[38]

---

36. The provision in Deut. 23:15-16 for allowing a runaway slave safe haven probably refers to foreign slaves fleeing to the military camp of Israel.
37. Given that female Hebrew slaves are not mentioned at this stage in the law (contrast Deut. 15:12 written 38 years later) we should probably understand the wife here to be a foreign slave belonging to the master. Although not stipulated in so many words, if a slave was given a wife by his master and chose not to remain as a permanent slave, that fact would not necessarily annul the marriage-bond. The young man would return to live with his parents, who more than likely lived in the same or a nearby village. His wife and children would be bound to serve their master, but this would not prevent communal living. At a later date the young man may even be able to purchase the freedom of his wife and children.
38. Deut. 15:12, however, also mentions the possibility that a Hebrew woman might end up in slavery.

A judge could also organise the sale of someone unable to pay a fine (cf. Exod. 22:3). The debt then had to be worked off. When the debt had been paid, the slave could go free. We may envisage a situation where the man unable to pay his debt could be sold (or, as here, sell a son) to a third party for a term of service equivalent to the debt owed. The price paid for the slave would go to the creditor and the slave would serve his purchaser for the required term of service.[39] But in cases of grave debt, God placed a limit on the number of years service the master might demand. This will have prevented wealthy citizens from loaning huge sums of money or property to high-risk clients. The maximum amount which could ever be recuperated was the equivalent of six years labour (in addition to any assets still held by the debtor).[40]

The law here concerns the debt-slavery of a male Hebrew. The following law addresses the sale of an unmarried (virgin) Hebrew female (Exod. 21:7-11) to be a wife. It would seem that it was not the norm for women to be sold into debt-slavery. If a woman was married, then her husband would ultimately be held responsible for any financial transactions. In 2 Kings 4:1 we see a situation where a creditor demands the children of a widow. The widow herself does not appear to be threatened with debt-slavery.

Voluntary permanent slavery

A Hebrew slave was also given the opportunity of *choosing* to remain with his master permanently. The situation envisaged in verse 5 is that of a debt-slave who has acquired a wife (and subsequent children) from his master. The picture is that of a single young man, presumably the original debtor's son, who was sold into slavery to pay his father's debt. During the course of his service his master has offered him a wife from among his slaves as an incentive to stay in his service.

---

39. This situation is not too far removed from judicial rulings in Western society whereby someone is required to pay off a debt by parting with a certain percentage of his earnings. The idea is that he be left enough money for himself to live by, but be compelled to pay off his debt with any surplus income.
40. It is interesting to contrast the *codex Hammurabi* (§117) which had a maximum of three years for debt-slavery. God's law takes the problem of indebtedness twice as seriously.

When the time of service has ended, the young man is free to choose to remain with his master instead of returning to his parents (who presumably still control the inherited land) and siblings. It is easy to see how such a situation could be attractive. The master was then to bring the slave to *hā-'elōhîm*, a word usually translated 'God' or 'gods' in the Bible, but it is sometimes used as an honorific title for judges given that they function in determining right and wrong. In Exodus 22:8 judges are certainly meant as *hā-'elōhîm* is followed by a plural – not a singular – verb (see further the discussion on that text). The interpretation 'judges' should, therefore, probably also be preferred here.[41] The slave was to be brought to the judges who would be expected to come to the master's home and bear witness to the fact that he voluntarily wished to become his master's permanent slave. The master would then drive an awl through his ear into the door or doorpost of his house (cf. Deut. 15:17). This symbolised the fact that the slave was henceforth *bound* in obedience to this house (cf. the Hebrew expression 'to give ear' meaning 'to obey'). It is the kind of physical sign that typically accompanied an oath ceremony. The slave is therefore pictured as swearing an oath before the judges as his ear is pierced into the door(post) of his master's house.

Slavery of a land-holder

In Deuteronomy 15:12-18 a similar law is given, however the scenario presupposed is slightly different. Here the debt-slave is not provided with a wife by his master, but the master is instructed, upon the maximum six years of service, to provide him with animals from his flock, grain from his threshing floor, and wine from his vat. The ex-slave is to be given a fresh start in society and not just thrown onto the street. The master is always to remember the compassion of Yhwh upon Israel when he set them free from the Egyptian slavery (cf. Exod.

---

41. The Septuagint interprets the phrase in terms of the master bringing the slave 'before the tribunal of God'. If the rendering 'God' is preferred, then the implication is that the slave would take an oath at the altar (*nb.* the sanctuary had not yet been built, cf. Exod. 21:14). The problem is then that the ceremony, which must occur at the door of the master's house (given that God's house does not exist at this point), is hereby separated from the oath and no longer concurrent with it.

3:21-22). The provision presupposes that the slave in *this* scenario holds the title to his inherited land. The master therefore enables him to work that land following upon his period of service. The option of becoming a permanent slave is still provided. It should be remembered that there will have been certain people who (through incompetence or other limitations) found it very difficult to provide themselves and their family with an income from their land. If they had been in debt slavery, this is an indication that they had already failed at least twice. An initial failure would have been followed by an interest-free loan. The second failure would have incurred the debt-slavery. If the period of service to the master had been satisfactory, a permanent service to him might seem more attractive than a third attempt at making one's own living.

Slavery when title to land has been lost

The slavery laws of Exodus 21 and Deuteronomy 15 are supplemented by the law of Leviticus 25:39-55. The laws of Exodus 21 and Deuteronomy 15 presuppose a form of debt slavery whereby the title to inherited land has not been lost. In Exodus 21 the slave is presupposed to be a son, who does not yet have title to any land. In Deuteronomy 15 he retains title to his land and is therefore given provisions to work it after his term of service. Leviticus 25 concerns laws related to the preservation of land in the families of Israel, particularly through the institution of the year of Jubilee. The slavery law in this chapter concerns a Hebrew who has become so poor that he is forced to part with his land and thus sell himself into slavery. Debt is here not the problem. The Hebrew envisaged has no means (i.e. land) with which to provide himself an income. We ought not to forget that Israel was very much an agricultural and farming community dependant on the land. The ancient economy had no job market such as modern Western economies. Men worked on their own land, had their own home business, and employed their own sons to work for them. Farmers could use day labourers in season, but such workers were employed on a daily basis and enjoyed no fixed income (cf. Matt. 20:1-15). If extra workers were needed, foreign slaves could be purchased. It was, therefore, catastrophic for a Hebrew to become so poor that he needed to part with all his land. He was then often forced to sell himself into slavery. He did not work to pay off a debt. He worked as a slave because there was no other way for him to survive in the society, that is, until his land could be returned to him in the Jubilee year (once every fifty years). Land in Israel was a part of the inheritance promised by Yʜwʜ to his people. It was never to be sold permanently, but only to be leased. Every Jubilee year the land was to revert back to the tribes and families to which it originally belonged. A Hebrew living as a slave because he had sold (i.e. leased) his land in poverty was to be released in the year of Jubilee when his land would be returned to him and he would receive a new opportunity for earning his own way in society. The law in Leviticus 25 stresses the fact that a Hebrew in this situation must not be treated harshly. He is to be thought of more as a hired labourer than a slave. Once again the master is to reflect upon the mercy of Yʜwʜ when he delivered the Israelites out of their harsh slavery in Egypt.

Elsewhere God warns his people not to forget mercy when dealing with problems of debt and debt-slavery (cf. Amos 2:6 and Neh. 5:5 and 8).

'Master' of a slave vs 'master' of a wife

An additional note on the terminology used in this law of Exodus 21 for 'master' and for 'husband' is warranted. In verse 3 the law speaks of the possibility that the slave is the 'husband' of a wife. The term used here for 'husband' is *baal*, the same word used for the god Baal. It literally means 'lord' or 'master', but is a common term in the Bible for the husband in a marriage relationship (e.g. Exod. 21:22; Deut. 24:4; 2 Sam. 11:26; Prov. 12:4; 31:11, 23, 28; Joel 1:8; cf. Isa. 54:5; Jer. 3:14; 31:32). It is directly related to the verb 'to marry' (*baal*) which means literally 'to become master of' (see, e.g. Deut. 21:13; 24:1; Isa. 62:5; Mal. 2:11). A wife is thus sometimes called 'the mastered one' (*bᵉulah*, cf. Isa. 54:1; 62:4-5; Gen. 20:3; Deut. 22:22). This marriage terminology reflects the biblical teaching of the man's headship in marriage (cf. Eph. 5:22-33).

The word for the master of the slave here is *adōn* which also means 'lord' and is often used as a title for God ('the Lord God').[42] Occasionally we find a wife addressing her husband with this honorific title, for example, Genesis 18:12; (cf. Jud. 19:26-27 [used by a concubine]; 1Kgs. 1:17 and Ps. 45:11 [used by the wife of the king]). 1 Peter 3:6 mentions the use of this honorific title by Sarah of Abraham to encourage Christian wives to respect the headship of their husbands.

Slavery and Egypt

In retrospect, we may ask why God chose to begin the list of judgments for his people with laws on slavery! The supplement to this law in Deuteronomy 15 as well as God's own reference to it by the mouth of the prophet Jeremiah make a direct connection between the deliverance out of the slavery in Egypt and the slave-law. The point is that Israelites are not to be kept as slaves permanently. Slave-owners should reflect upon God's deliverance of them (or their forefathers) from permanent slavery. YHWH accuses the slave-owners in Jeremiah's time of neglecting this law and pronounces his judgment as a result (see Jer. 34:8-22).

The slave law and Herod the Great

Finally, it is interesting to note that Josephus, in his account of the reign of Herod the Great, notes that he abandoned this law.[43] Given the recent civil strife leading up to his coup it is not surprising that Josephus records that he needed to deal with an inordinate increase in house-breaking. He enacted that thieves be sold into slavery *outside* the kingdom. This meant that such thieves essentially became slaves for life to non-Jewish masters. Josephus attributes this contravention of Jewish law as partly to blame for the charges made against him and the general disapproval of the people of his reign.

---

42. Later Jewish tradition uses slightly different vowels in the spelling of this word when it is used of God in order to make clear the distinction between the divine and human title.
43. *Antiq.* 16.1-5.

Text

Καὶ ταῦτα τὰ δικαιώματα, ἃ παραθήσεις ἐνώπιον αὐτῶν. ² ἐὰν κτήσῃ παῖδα Ἑβραῖον, ἓξ ἔτη δουλεύσει σοι· τῷ δὲ ἔτει τῷ ἑβδόμῳ ἀπελεύσεται ἐλεύθερος δωρεάν. ³ ἐὰν αὐτὸς μόνος εἰσέλθῃ, καὶ μόνος ἐξελεύσεται· ἐὰν δὲ γυνὴ συνεισέλθῃ μετ' αὐτοῦ, καὶ ἡ γυνὴ ἐξελεύσεται μετ' αὐτοῦ. ⁴ ἐὰν δὲ ὁ κύριος δῷ αὐτῷ γυναῖκα, καὶ τέκῃ αὐτῷ υἱοὺς ἢ θυγατέρας, ἡ γυνὴ καὶ τὰ παιδία ἔσται τῷ κυρίῳ αὐτοῦ, αὐτὸς δὲ μόνος ἐξελεύσεται. ⁵ ἐὰν δὲ ἀποκριθεὶς εἴπῃ ὁ παῖς Ἠγάπηκα τὸν κύριόν μου καὶ τὴν γυναῖκα καὶ τὰ παιδία, οὐκ ἀποτρέχω ἐλεύθερος· ⁶ προσάξει αὐτὸν ὁ κύριος αὐτοῦ πρὸς τὸ κριτήριον τοῦ θεοῦ, καὶ τότε προσάξει αὐτὸν ἐπὶ τὴν θύραν ἐπὶ τὸν σταθμόν, καὶ τρυπήσει αὐτοῦ ὁ κύριος τὸ οὖς τῷ ὀπητίῳ, καὶ δουλεύσει αὐτῷ εἰς τὸν αἰῶνα.	וְאֵלֶּה הַמִּשְׁפָּטִים אֲשֶׁר תָּשִׂים לִפְנֵיהֶם: ² כִּי תִקְנֶה עֶבֶד עִבְרִי שֵׁשׁ שָׁנִים יַעֲבֹד וּבַשְּׁבִעִת יֵצֵא לַחָפְשִׁי חִנָּם: ³ אִם־בְּגַפּוֹ יָבֹא בְּגַפּוֹ יֵצֵא אִם־בַּעַל אִשָּׁה הוּא וְיָצְאָה אִשְׁתּוֹ עִמּוֹ: ⁴ אִם־אֲדֹנָיו יִתֶּן־לוֹ אִשָּׁה וְיָלְדָה־לוֹ בָנִים אוֹ בָנוֹת הָאִשָּׁה וִילָדֶיהָ תִּהְיֶה לַאדֹנֶיהָ וְהוּא יֵצֵא בְגַפּוֹ: ⁵ וְאִם־אָמֹר יֹאמַר הָעֶבֶד אָהַבְתִּי אֶת־אֲדֹנִי אֶת־אִשְׁתִּי וְאֶת־בָּנָי לֹא אֵצֵא חָפְשִׁי: ⁶ וְהִגִּישׁוֹ אֲדֹנָיו אֶל־הָאֱלֹהִים וְהִגִּישׁוֹ אֶל־הַדֶּלֶת אוֹ אֶל־הַמְּזוּזָה וְרָצַע אֲדֹנָיו אֶת־אָזְנוֹ בַּמַּרְצֵעַ וַעֲבָדוֹ לְעֹלָם:
חָפְשִׁי, set free חִנָּם, adv. without giving or taking compensation (חֵן + adv. ◌ָם) גַּף, body (hapax legomenon), cf. גּוּפָה, corpse⁴⁴	רצע, Qal to pierce through (hapax legomenon) מַרְצֵעַ, awl / strong pointed needle (used only here and Dt. 15:17)

---

44. גּוּפָה is cognate to Jewish Aramaic גּוּף ('body / self') and is post-exilic Hebrew. It is more likely that גַּף is directly cognate to Aramaic.

21:1
וְאֵלֶּה הַמִּשְׁפָּטִים / Καὶ ταῦτα τὰ δικαιώματα

The noun δικαίωμα in the sense of 'decree' or 'ordinance' is typical of Jewish Greek.

21:2
עִבְרִי / Εβραῖον

The term comes from the verb עבר ('to go on one's way', 'to pass through') and was first used of Abram in Gen. 14:13 as a 'traveller'. Here it has become a designation of ethnicity and thus remains untranslated in Greek.

יַעֲבֹד / δουλεύσει σοι

The LXX (as well as the Sam. Pent.) read: יַעַבְדְךָ. The verb should probably be understood as a jussive ('he may serve'). Six years is a maximum term of service. See the main commentary.

ἀπελεύσεται

It is interesting that, although the technical term for slave manumission (ἀποτρέχω) is used later on in this pericope, it is not used here.

21:3
בְּגַפּוֹ / αὐτὸς μόνος

Lit. 'in his body' = alone. The expression is only used here. Regular Hebrew would be לְבַדּוֹ 'alone' (lit. 'to his portion').

אִם־בְּגַפּוֹ יָבֹא בְּגַפּוֹ יֵצֵא אִם־בַּעַל אִשָּׁה הוּא וְיָצְאָה

Note that the 'waw of apodosis' (usually translated 'then') is not used when the apodosis does not begin with a verb, cf. Jouön/Muraoka §176d. Therefore there is no waw in 21:3a (cf. 21:4).

אִם־בַּעַל אִשָּׁה הוּא / ἐὰν δὲ γυνὴ συνεισέλθῃ μετ' αὐτοῦ

The rather free rendering here may have to do with the fact that under Greek law and thus also in Hellenistic kingdoms marriages of slaves were not formally recognised. Jews, at the time this translation was made, were part of such Hellenistic kingdoms. The translator has therefore removed the technical terms for marriage.

21:4
אִם־אֲדֹנָיו יִתֶּן־לוֹ / ἐὰν δὲ ὁ κύριος δῷ αὐτῷ

With very few exceptions, the noun אָדוֹן with suffix always takes a plural form (but contrast v.5), usually categorised (when with a singular verb) as a plural of majesty. Note also that, although the Greek text is quite literal, there is a general tendency in Greek to add a connecting particle to any new sentence. This tendency is especially prominent after ἐάν beginning a sentence, wholly so in the laws of the Book of the Covenant. It is therefore not always easy to tell whether ἐὰν δέ suggests that the Greek translator had a Hebrew *waw* before him.

הָאִשָּׁה וִילָדֶיהָ תִּהְיֶה

When the verb *follows* a plurality of subjects we would normally expect a plural verb (verbs *preceding* a plurality of subjects generally show the number of the first subject only). Jouön/Muraoka §150p suggests that in this case we should see the *waw* as indicating accompaniment.

לַאדֹנֶיהָ / τῷ κυρίῳ αὐτοῦ

The reading of the LXX (לַאדֹנָיו) is supported by the Sam. Pent.

21:5

וְאִם־אָמֹר יֹאמַר

The prepositive infinitive absolute is commonly used for emphasis, but in conditional clauses it may suggest an unlikely possibility, cf. Jouön/Muraoka §123g.

אָהַבְתִּי / Ἠγάπηκα

The LXX has rendered the originally stative Hebrew verb, which is thus used in the perfect with a present meaning, with a true Greek perfect ('I have come to love' and thus 'I love').

אֶת־אֲדֹנִי אֶת־אִשְׁתִּי וְאֶת־בָּנָי / τὸν κύριόν μου καὶ τὴν γυναῖκα καὶ τὰ παιδία

The LXX has an extra copulative, which may have been omitted in the Hebrew text by haplography. The omission in the LXX of the personal pronouns to the wife and children may also be due to haplography, although strictly speaking they are not needed in Greek (the definite article is sufficient).

οὐκ ἀποτρέχω ἐλεύθερος

Note that the verb ἀποτρέχω is the technical term for the manumitted departure of slaves in Greek.

21:6

וְהִגִּישׁוֹ

The verb נגשׁ is *telic*, in other words, it means 'to approach' in the sense of actually reaching one's destination.[45]

אֶל־הָאֱלֹהִים / πρὸς τὸ κριτήριον τοῦ θεοῦ

The LXX here gives us an interpretation. See further in the main commentary. The ensuing τότε is probably also interpretative. The translator may be thinking of a doorpost at the temple.

אוֹ אֶל־הַמְּזוּזָה / ἐπὶ τὸν σταθμόν

It may just be that the LXX interpreted או אל as an example of dittography (as if אל אל).

אֶת־אָזְנוֹ / τὸ οὖς

In Greek the definite article is sufficient to suggest '*his* ear'. It seems unlikely that the LXX read אֶת־הָאֹזֶן.

בַּמַּרְצֵעַ / τῷ ὀπητίῳ

Jouön/Muraoka §137m states: "A thing which is not perceived as determinate by the writer or by the person who is addressed is sometimes specifically determinate by itself; therefore the noun takes, or can take, the article. This use of the article is characteristic of Hebrew and rather frequent. It can only be translated in English by *a*, sometimes by *a certain*." In this case the noun is determinate because it refers not just to any awl, but that awl which is taken for this purpose.

לְעֹלָם

The word עוֹלָם is often translated 'eternity' in our English Bibles and this can give the impression that 'eternity' is the specific meaning of the word. In fact that word simply means 'long(est) or farthest time' and it can refer to a long time either forwards (in the future) or backwards (into the past). How long a duration is meant is entirely according to the context, but the word signifies the longest time available (not a long time after which other periods of time could occur). The translation 'eternal' therefore gives a wrong impression. See Jenni[1], 236.

---

45. Jenni[4], 219.

21:7-11

Treatment of a Hebrew girl sold as slave-wife

Translation

⁷ And when someone sells his daughter as a slave-wife, then she shall not go out as slaves go out.

⁸ If she is no good in the eyes of her master who has designated her for himself,⁴⁶ then he shall allow her to be redeemed.⁴⁷ He is not authorised to sell her to a foreign people since he has dealt treacherously with her.

⁹ And if he designates her for his son, he shall treat her according to the legal judgment for daughters.

¹⁰ If he takes another wife for himself, then he shall not reduce her meat, her clothing or her conjugal rights.

---

46. The Masoretic text of v.8a reads: "If she is no good in the eyes of her master who has not designated her, then he shall allow her to be redeemed." Most translations correctly emend the 'not' (*l'ō* / לא) of the Massoretic text in v.8 to the prepositional phrase 'to him' (*lō* / לו), a reading already found in the LXX. This reading maintains a parallel word-order in vs.8-9. The Massoretic text would assume that the master-husband desires to sell her off before having designated her either to himself or to his son. This reading, besides loosening the parallel with v.9, begs the question why he would be said to have 'dealt treacherously with her'.
47. The phrase (translated literally) 'and he shall cause her to be redeemed' should not be read as part of the protasis ('if' clause) translating v.8 as follows: "If she is no good in the eyes of her master who has designated her for himself and he allows her to be redeemed, then he is not authorised to sell her to a foreign people since he has dealt treacherously with her." This translation would make the verb 'to cause to be redeemed' wrongly synonymous with the verb 'to sell'.

[11] And if he does not do these three things for her, then she shall go out without payment of money.

Commentary

A cursory reading of this law is likely to conjure up a picture of a wealthy man lusting after a pretty girl on the slave market whom he then purchases as a bed-fellow. Further reflection reveals a totally different picture. The law is indeed placed here because it also has to do with a form of slavery, but the nature of the slavery is quite different. The law treats the purchase of a girl who is to be set aside as a wife, either for the purchaser or for his son. Verse 7 lets us know that this case is different to the preceding law. The girl is not free to go after six years 'service', for she is to be a wife. This much is clear both from what follows in verses 9-10 as well as from the terminology used. The word for female slave in verse 7 indicates that the girl is to be a wife either to her master (or a member of his household) or to another slave. It is to be noted that Hebrew has two distinct terms for female slaves, one for a married female slave (*'āmāh*) and one for a non-married female slave (*shiphchāh*). In Israel, girls were not normally sold as working slaves. Non-married female slaves were usually either foreigners or girls who had been born into slavery. They were used as handmaids for the lady of the house, not the master.

As we shall see, this law should be considered part of the poor-laws in Israel, that is, a law designed to alleviate conditions of poverty.

The presupposition of the two laws regarding the sale of children (Exod. 21:2-11) appears to be that one's first recourse in times of financial need would be the sale of a son for a fixed time period. When this is not possible, one may consider the sale of a daughter, but daughters may not be sold into working service. They are only to be sold into marriage.

To understand something of the necessity of this law, we need to remember that at that time it was customary for a wife-to-be to receive a handsome dowry. This customary dowry payment (which itself is not further regulated in God's law) was not a payment made to the girl's parents by the suitor, but a payment from the girl's own parents to the girl herself (cf. 1 Kgs 9:16; Mic. 1:13-14). Here the parents receive money from the suitor given that their daughter is being sold as a slave-wife, as this law makes clear.[48]

Parents reduced to poverty might 'sell' their daughter into marriage, instead of giving her away (cf. Neh. 5:5). It is obvious that this would be a last resort for parents, for their daughter is, in a real sense, demeaned. She no longer has the independent wealth that would be hers by way of a dowry. Furthermore, she has the status of a slave-wife. She, therefore, has no right to divorce her husband-master in a normal way and her husband-master has the ability to cancel the promised marriage on virtually any grounds before the actual consummation of the marriage (see below). We should, however, also consider the fact that it would be socially demeaning for the husband-master to have as his wife a daughter who had been purchased from a poor family instead of a free girl with independent wealth (via her dowry). This would lead us to consider that the man who purchases a wife in this way, is at least partially motivated by a desire to assist a family reduced to poverty, despite the implications for his own social standing.

The law in question protects the rights of a girl who is sold in this way by her parents. There are three separate legal judgments.

Judgment 1: Cancellation of the promised marriage

In the first judgment we are introduced to the case where the purchaser has appointed the slave-girl to be his own wife, but she is 'no-good in his eyes' and he elects to cancel the promised marriage. A few remarks on the terminology used are appropriate. The law in Exod.

---

48. It is unclear from Scripture whether it was normal custom for a suitor to give a payment to the parents of his bride. Texts such as Gen. 24:53 may suggest this, although such 'gifts' may not have been considered to be an actual payment (contractual terminology such as the verb מכר is not used). If such a custom was normal, one must ask what the financial benefit to the parents would be in contractually *selling* their daughter (the non-payment of a dowry?). If such a payment were not customary, then Saul's demands on David (1 Sam. 18:25) could be understood in the light of this law. Saul demeans both his own daughter and David by making him purchase Michal as his wife.

21 speaks of her being 'bad' (*ra'ah*) in his eyes. The way the Hebrew is worded shows that this would be unexpected.[49] The word refers to 'badness', whether moral or otherwise. When referring to non-moral 'badness' it usually implies some kind of great misfortune or calamity. In other words, it is quite a strong word. The terminology used for the engagement contract of a slave-wife (lit., 'designation') is distinct from that used for the engagement contract of a free wife (lit. 'engagement / betrothal').[50] It is unclear whether the engagement to a free wife could also be broken before the actual wedding (and consummation). In any case, Deuteronomy 21:23-24 treats sexual activity with an engaged woman as adultery. The point of this first legal judgment is that, in case of cancellation of the marriage, she is to be given the right of redemption. Her parents, or other next of kin, may buy her back. She is under no circumstances to be sold to a foreigner whereby she might be taken outside of the covenant community. Her status as a covenant child of God is hereby safeguarded. This may mean that if her next of kin do not wish to redeem her, she may be sold to another Israelite. In this way the purchaser may recuperate something of his costs. The imposed restrictions are given "since he has dealt treacherously with her", in other words, he has broken the contracted marriage-to-be. The wording makes it clear that while it is possible for him to break the contracted marriage, it is nevertheless considered to be morally reprehensible. The 'treachery' lies in the fact that the purchaser has reneged upon his contractual obligation to marry the girl. Given that in Israelite society it was not customary for a man to have a non-married female slave, he will now need to have her redeemed or sell her to someone else. The law presupposes that the master in question is not yet married and thus he cannot give the girl as a slave to his wife. The right of redemption enables the family to buy her back so that she may yet be married to someone else and thus bear children.

Although some interpreters suggest that the text implies that the purchaser finds the girl disagreeable after having taken away her virginity, upon reflection this interpretation is impossible. Were that

---

49. A nominal clause is used, see the textual commentary.
50. For a slave-wife the verb יעד, *Qal* 'to designate' is used, for a free wife it is the verb ארש, *Piel* 'to become engaged / betrothed'.

the case, there would be no need for her to be redeemed. The law goes on to state that if she is set aside (i.e. no more conjugal relations are forthcoming) she is free to walk away without payment.[51]

Parallels

A different, and yet in many ways parallel, law in Deuteronomy 21:10-14 concerns the treatment of a slave-girl captured in war who is taken as a wife. Both here and in Exodus 21 it is clear that the husband-master has the right to annul the promised marriage. However in the case of a girl captured in war who was not paid for, the master-husband may not sell her, but must let her go wherever she pleases. In other words she may choose to return to her homeland or to settle in Israel, which would probably mean that she would need to sell herself back into slavery, but without a marriage. The point is that, having 'humbled' her, he may not make a profit from her. The condition for annulment in both cases is worded differently. In the case of a Hebrew slave-wife (Exodus 21), there must be some (serious) 'badness'. In the case of a foreign girl captured in war, it may merely be that the husband-master finds that she is not 'pleasing in his eyes'.

A parallel case is presented in Genesis 21:8-14, where Abraham sends Hagar away without selling her. She is specifically said to have the status of a slave-wife (*'āmāh*, Gen. 21:10), although Abraham had received her as a gift from Sarah (Gen. 16).

Judgment 2: A girl purchased for marriage to one's son

The second judgment concerns the situation where the purchaser gives the slave-girl to be a wife for his son. In this case she is to be treated "according to the law of daughters". Precisely what this entails is not spelled out. The law suggests that the master who purchased her must treat her as if she were his own daughter whom he was giving away in marriage. This seems to mean that he ought to provide her with a dowry and that she be given the status of a free-wife, not that of a slave-wife.

---

51. Of interest in this respect is Sirach 25:26 which advises the man whose wife will not do his will to "cut her off from his flesh", that is, to refuse her conjugal relations (the quoted phrase is not divorce terminology).

Judgment 3: Conditions for divorce

The third judgment concerns the situation where the husband-master of the slave-girl, who was sold by her parents, acquires another wife next to her. This judgment protects the rights of the slave-girl as a wife. Just because she was *purchased*, she is not to be treated any less a wife. Her rights to food,[52] shelter and conjugal relations[53] are to be upheld. If these things are withheld or reduced, then she has the right to walk away from her master-husband. No payment or redemption is required. She may go free and thereby effect a divorce. Her right to conjugal relations should be interpreted as the right to bear children, who would then have a moral responsibility to care for her in times of trouble or in old age as well as the right to inheritance. It is important to note that this law presumes that a girl purchased as a wife would be, in the first instance, the only wife of the husband-master. Any notion of concubinage is excluded.

An historical application of this law

An interesting example of a modified execution of this law is found in the book of Ruth where Naomi, who wishes to give Ruth away in marriage, is not in a position to give her a dowry. She elects to sell the land belonging to her through her deceased husband Elimelech and to 'sell' Ruth along with it. Because there is no male heir this sale is permanent and therefore needs to be bought within the clan via a 'redeemer'. In this way Ruth, although 'sold' into marriage, will be able to raise offspring to inherit the land in the name of Elimelech and his son (Ruth's former husband) Mahlon.

---

52. The text specifically refers to 'meat' (שְׁאֵר) which implies a normal full diet.
53. The 1st – 2nd century AD rabbi Eliezer (ben Hyrcanus) gave the following ruling, illustrating that the principle of conjugal rights had to be applied differently in different situations: "'The sexual duty of which the Torah speaks [Ex. 21:10]: (1) those without work [of independent means]—every day; (2) workers—twice a week; (3) ass drivers–once a week; (4) camel drivers— once in thirty days; (5) sailors—once in six months,' the words of R. Eliezer." Mishnah, *Ketuboth* 5.6.

Text

⁷ ἐὰν δέ τις ἀποδῶται τὴν ἑαυτοῦ θυγατέρα οἰκέτιν, οὐκ ἀπελεύσεται ὥσπερ ἀποτρέχουσιν αἱ δοῦλαι. ⁸ ἐὰν μὴ εὐαρεστήσῃ τῷ κυρίῳ αὐτῆς ἣν αὑτῷ καθωμολογήσατο, ἀπολυτρώσει αὐτήν· ἔθνει δὲ ἀλλοτρίῳ οὐ κύριός ἐστιν πωλεῖν αὐτήν, ὅτι ἠθέτησεν ἐν αὐτῇ. ⁹ ἐὰν δὲ τῷ υἱῷ καθομολογήσηται αὐτήν, κατὰ τὸ δικαίωμα τῶν θυγατέρων ποιήσει αὐτῇ. ¹⁰ ἐὰν δὲ ἄλλην λάβῃ ἑαυτῷ, τὰ δέοντα καὶ τὸν ἱματισμὸν καὶ τὴν ὁμιλίαν αὐτῆς οὐκ ἀποστερήσει. ¹¹ ἐὰν δὲ τὰ τρία ταῦτα μὴ ποιήσῃ αὐτῇ, ἐξελεύσεται δωρεὰν ἄνευ ἀργυρίου.	⁷וְכִי־יִמְכֹּר אִישׁ אֶת־בִּתּוֹ לְאָמָה לֹא תֵצֵא כְּצֵאת הָעֲבָדִים: ⁸ אִם־רָעָה בְּעֵינֵי אֲדֹנֶיהָ אֲשֶׁר־לֹא יְעָדָהּ וְהֶפְדָּהּ לְעַם נָכְרִי לֹא־יִמְשֹׁל לְמָכְרָהּ בְּבִגְדוֹ־בָהּ: ⁹ וְאִם־לִבְנוֹ יִיעָדֶנָּה כְּמִשְׁפַּט הַבָּנוֹת יַעֲשֶׂה־לָּהּ: ¹⁰ אִם־אַחֶרֶת יִקַּח־לוֹ שְׁאֵרָהּ כְּסוּתָהּ וְעֹנָתָהּ לֹא יִגְרָע: ¹¹ וְאִם־שְׁלָשׁ־אֵלֶּה לֹא יַעֲשֶׂה לָהּ וְיָצְאָה חִנָּם אֵין כָּסֶף:

ἀποδίδωμι, to give back; *Mid.* to sell	καθομολογέω, to promise, engage, vow
יעד, *Qal* to designate	אַחֵר, *fem.* אַחֶרֶת other
פדה, *Qal* to buy out / redeem; *Hiph.* to allow to be ransomed (only used here)	שְׁאֵר, body, flesh *and therefore* meat (as food)
בגד, *Qal* to deal treacherously with + בְּ	כְּסוּת, covering, clothing
	עֹנָה, sexual intercourse
	גרע, *Qal* to trim, to cut down

21:7

יִמְכֹּר / ἀποδῶται

The LXX rendering (ἀποδίδωμι) may imply that the girl is given as a payment for debt, although the verb ἀποδίδωμι in the middle voice also functions as a regular verb 'to sell'. The Hebrew verb simply means 'to sell' without any suggestion as to the reason for selling.

In v.8 the LXX uses πωλέω ('to sell') to translate מכר, so the use of ἀποδίδωμι here may suggest a deliberate interpretation.

לְאָמָה / οἰκέτιν

An אָמָה is a married female slave. An unmarried female slave is a שִׁפְחָה, who was normally restricted in service to the lady of the house. The LXX assumes that any female slave will have been working in the house and not the field.

לֹא תֵצֵא

Note that the '*waw* of apodosis' (usually translated 'then') is not used when the apodosis does not begin with a verb, cf. Jouön/Muraoka §176d, n.

כְּצֵאת הָעֲבָדִים / ὥσπερ ἀποτρέχουσιν αἱ δοῦλαι

The LXX seems to have understood the feminine form עבדות, which is not used at all otherwise. The verb ἀποτρέχω is the technical term for the manumitted departure of slaves in Greek.

21:8

אִם־רָעָה בְּעֵינֵי אֲדֹנֶיהָ

Note the use of the nominal clause as opposed to the (rather common) verbal equivalent (e.g. וַיֵּרַע בְּעֵינֵי). The verbal clause would have implied that 'badness' naturally belongs to such slave-wives. The nominal clause suggests that this slave-wife, whom you would not necessarily think of as 'bad', is in fact such. רָעָה does not necessarily imply moral 'badness', but is a fairly strong word, usually implying great misfortune or calamity.

אֲשֶׁר־לֹא יְעָדָהּ / ἣν αὑτῷ καθωμολογήσατο

The LXX reads לוֹ and is followed by the ESV and NKJV. Indeed, comparing the word-order of the parallel clauses, this reading makes complete sense. Besides, if he has not designated her, why has he dealt treacherously with her?

וְהֶפְדָּהּ

While פדה *(Qal)* is the general term for 'to redeem' / 'to buy out', גאל is the term used in family relations.

לְעַם נָכְרִי / ἔθνει δὲ ἀλλοτρίῳ

The LXX may have read: וּלְעַם נָכְרִי.

לֹא־יִמְשֹׁל

The verb means 'to have authority'. When, as commonly, used with בְּ it means 'to have authority over' in the sense of ruling. Here it is used with לְ in the sense of having authority to do something.

בְּבִגְדוֹ / ἠθέτησεν ἐν αὐτῇ

The unusual spelling of the infin. cstr. with suffix (we should expect בְּבִגְדוֹ) is due to the analogy with the segholate noun בֶּגֶד ('garment', with suffix בִּגְדוֹ), cf. Joüon/Muraoka §65b. In regular Greek and also in the New Testament the verb ἀθετέω is transitive. The LXX, under the influence of Hebrew, tends to treat it as intransitive requiring a preposition such as ἐν or εἰς.

21:10

אִם־אַחֶרֶת / ἐὰν δὲ ἄλλην

On the question of a copulative, see the note to 21:4

שְׁאֵרָהּ / τὰ δέοντα

The Greek refers to 'the things that are needed / necessary', and is elsewhere used in the LXX for 'rations' (translating לֶחֶם in the sense of 'food' or 'rations'), cf. LXX Exod. 16:22; 1 Kgs 5:2. It is noteworthy that the phrase ἐπιχορηγεῖν τὰ δέοντα is used in the papyri for the giving of gifts in marriage contracts. In fact, at BGU 1 183 (line 7), a contract dated to AD 85 outlining bridal gifts from a widow to her married children, mentions the conditions for the continuing cohabitation of the married couple as: [τὰ δέοντα] πάντα καὶ τὸν ἱματισ[μὸν καὶ τὰ ἄλλα ὅσα] καθ[ήκει] γυναικὶ γαμετῇ.

שְׁאֵרָהּ כְּסוּתָהּ וְעֹנָתָהּ לֹא יִגְרָע

Note the omission of אֶת־ with each of the three direct objects, which is common when a direct object precedes its verb.

21:12-17

CASE LAWS
LAWS WITH PENAL SANCTIONS: 2. ASSAULT

Murder/manslaughter, parent-child crimes

Translation

¹² One who strikes a person such that he dies shall surely be killed. ¹³ But with respect to someone who did not lie in wait, yet God caused it to happen to his hands, I will set for you a place where he may flee. ¹⁴ But when someone becomes angry against his neighbour to kill him with cunning, then (even) from my altar you may take him to die.

¹⁵ And one who strikes his father or his mother shall surely be killed.

¹⁶ And one who steals a person, whether he sells him or he is found in his possession[54], shall surely be killed.

¹⁷ And one who declares his father or his mother to be accursed shall surely be killed.

Commentary

The following series of laws are connected together in several ways. The fact that they all begin with the subject and not the verb and are

---

54. Lit. 'in his hand'.

connected by the simple conjunction (*waw*) indicates that they belong together. This word-order (conjunction – noun – verb) is generally used in Hebrew to indicate circumstantial clauses. The first law sets forth the more general overarching crime of striking a person so that he dies. This law is further divided into murder versus manslaughter. The ensuing laws, which are also capital crimes, concern striking one's parents, kidnapping a child for slavery and calling upon God to strike one's parents.

Murder / manslaughter

This law deals with the killing of a fellow human being and the distinction between murder and manslaughter. Anyone who kills another person by accident may flee to a designated place where he can be considered safe. It should be noted that, although the concept of a place of asylum was common to the ancient world, its restriction to those guilty of *accidental manslaughter* was unique to Israel. Places of asylum in the ancient world were mostly holy places, for example, temples. In Israel too it was permissible to flee to the temple – that much is clear from verse 14 where it is stated that a murderer may be taken away from the altar (implying that one who committed manslaughter was safe there, cf. 1 Kgs 1:50ff; 2:28ff; Ps. 27:5). And this is what is unique in God's law for his people. For in the ancient world (even in the time of the New Testament), someone who had fled to a place of asylum *was always safe no matter what he had done*. God's law makes a distinction between manslaughter and murder in respect to the right of asylum. Asylum is restricted to manslaughter.

It may surprise us, however, to learn that God defines the distinction between murder and manslaughter in a slightly different way than many modern nations or even other ancient civilisations. It is clear from this law that anyone who intentionally kills another person (i.e. in an illegal manner[55]) is guilty of murder and warrants the death penalty. But how does God define manslaughter (killing without intent)? The text speaks of someone who did not lie in wait for the other person,

---

55. Examples of legal killings are warfare, striking a thief caught in the act at night (Exod. 22:2), or rightful execution of one's duty as a blood-avenger (see below).

but God let him fall into his hand. In Numbers 35:22-24 a couple of examples are given:

> *But if he pushed him suddenly without enmity, or hurled anything on him without lying in wait or used a stone that could cause death, and without seeing him dropped it on him, so that he died, though he was not his enemy and did not seek his harm, then the congregation shall judge between the manslayer and the avenger of blood, in accordance with these rules.*

In such cases the person is cleared of a murder-charge. He may stay in a city of refuge. Manslaughter is, however, here defined in terms of *no intent to harm* and not *no intent to kill*. This is clear from the preceding verses defining murder (Num. 35:20-21):

> *And if he pushed him out of hatred or hurled something at him, lying in wait, so that he died, or in enmity struck him down with his hand, so that he died, then he who struck the blow shall be put to death. He is a murderer. The avenger of blood shall put the murderer to death when he meets him.*

Murder is the killing of a person as a result of premeditated intent to harm. It may not have been one's intent to actually kill the person, but if he dies, then one must pay the penalty, an irrevocable death sentence.[56] This means that if someone accidentally killed a person, the only thing the prosecution needed to prove was *intent to harm*. If that person had demonstrably hated the victim, he could end up in a tight spot.

It is against this background that the Lord Jesus states that feelings of hate towards one's neighbour are in God's eyes tantamount to murder.

> *You have heard that it was said to those of old, 'You shall not murder; and whoever murders will be liable to judgment.' But I say to you that everyone who is angry with his brother will be liable to judgment; whoever insults his brother will be liable to the council; and whoever says, 'You fool!' will be liable to the hell of fire.* (Matt. 5:21-22)

---

56. In contrast, the *codex Hammurabi* distinguishes manslaughter and murder in terms of *intent to kill* not *intent to harm* (see §§ 206-208).

If it was clear that you had killed someone, then evidence that you called him names in hatred may have been enough to convict you of murder in certain circumstances. Jesus states that this in itself is sufficient to warrant God's punishment, for God is interested in the state of the human heart. In God's law, murder is defined in terms of the tragic results of feelings of enmity.

If enmity or intent to harm could not be proven, then the person who caused the death could in Israel flee to a city of refuge. The idea of such areas of asylum is strange to the modern Western mind. And yet we ought to realise that such places of asylum existed in Europe right up until the time of the Reformation, when they were generally abolished.

Cities of refuge

The biblical system of cities of refuge is worked out in more detail in Numbers 35:9-34; Deuteronomy 4:41-43; 19:1-13 and Joshua 20:1-9. It is only hinted at here in Exodus 21 and the suggestion is made that at least God's altar may function as such a place of asylum (the law suggests that this is self-evident). The system of cities of refuge was to work as follows: If you had accidentally killed someone, or even if you had committed a murder and yet because of the circumstances wanted a judicial trial, you were to flee to a city of refuge. Six such cities were to be provided in the various regions of Israel. These were Levitical cities and thus places where there was no question of land being bound to any particular family. This was important, because if the judges found that the death was indeed caused by accident, then you would be given a place to live in the city. Here you would have to remain until the death of the high priest. In a Levitical city, a house could be given away without the complications of property rights which would revert in the year of Jubilee (cf. Lev. 25:10).

If, however, you fled to such a city for refuge, the elders of that city had to first ascertain that your application was genuine (Josh. 20:4). They would be concerned to avoid having to supply lodging to anyone who happened by. After you were admitted to the city, you would have to await the outcome of a judicial inquiry. In Deuteronomy 19 we learn that it was the task of the elders in the region where the killing occurred to investigate the matter. If murder was proven (on the basis of at least two witnesses), you would be removed from the city of refuge and given over to the blood-avenger whose task it was to apply the death penalty.

This system which God appointed was, as mentioned above, quite different from the system common in the ancient world. Firstly, outside of Israel no one was *given* lodging if he fled to a recognised place of refuge / asylum. You would have to find your own place to stay. Secondly, if you reached a place of asylum in the ancient world you were *guaranteed* safety for as long as you remained there. No judicial process could extract you from that place – even if it was proven that you were guilty of the most horrendous crimes. Anyone could flee to such a place of asylum, no matter what crime he had committed. This will have meant that such cities (outside of Israel) in the ancient world could easily become societies of criminals. Anyone scared of the consequences of his crimes could flee there and be safe. During the Roman Imperium the evils of this system were generally known and often discussed in the Senate at Rome.[57] But they could do little to change the situation. What we don't often realise is the fact that the great city of Ephesus, where Paul worked for two years at preaching the Gospel, was just such a place of asylum – a refuge for all manner of criminals!

God's law regulated matters differently in Israel. Firstly, cities of refuge were only to provide refuge for those who had committed manslaughter (without intent to harm). It is to be noted that the laws in question make no mention of a distinction between manslaughter due to negligence versus manslaughter due to pure accident. The basic principles of God's law provide that harm done due to negligence requires restitution. This would suggest that there would have been opportunity for the family of the deceased to sue for damages in the case of manslaughter due to negligence. Secondly, if the court of elders

---

57. The problem had become particularly acute in the reign of Emperor Tiberius (AD 14-37) when such cities with asylum status in the Empire had become havens to all kinds of criminals. Even criminal slaves were safe there.

found that the accused was guilty of murder, he had to be removed to receive his punishment.

The system of cities of refuge remained in the civilised world, even after the Christianisation of the Roman Empire. After all, God's law also spoke of such cities. By that time the six Levitical cities had long disappeared. In Christian lands, churches were declared to be places of refuge. Most churches in these times owned considerable tracts of land where applicants for refuge could be put to work. But in the course of time this system began to be seriously misused. It was not propagated according to the rules of God's law, but according to what had been the practice in the former Roman Empire. Known criminals were protected by the church from any legal proceedings against them. It was because of this misuse that the principle of using churches as places of refuge was abandoned in the time of the Protestant Reformation.

One question remains: Why was it necessary to live in a city of refuge if you had killed someone by accident? Is this not a serious breech of one's personal freedom? To understand this, we need to pay some attention to the institution of the blood-avenger.

The 'blood-redeemer'

We ought to realise at the outset that the biblical institution of the blood-avenger had nothing to do with vigilante justice. In the first place, the word itself is not very accurately translated for the biblical expression literally means 'redeemer of blood'. Spilt blood has to be atoned for, and *that* is the concern of God's law. We read in Numbers 35:33 ...

> You shall not pollute the land in which you live, for blood pollutes the land, and no atonement can be made for the land for the blood that is shed in it, except by the blood of the one who shed it.

God's law is not concerned about the personal vengeance of a particular family, but about the setting right of a violent crime which desecrates the land – a land which God himself has chosen as his dwelling place. That spilt blood cries out to God was already clear as far back as Genesis 4:10 where God said to Cain, "The voice of your brother's blood is crying to me from the ground". God put it to Noah in these terms:

> *Whoever sheds the blood of man, by man shall his blood be shed, for God made man in his own image.* (Gen. 9:6)

Spilt blood cries out to be atoned, and this atonement is the task of the *blood-redeemer*. He must mete out the appropriate penalty for this crime and thus render justice.[58] He must concern himself with God's justice, not private retribution for his family. The *blood-redeemer* was the closest adult male in the family of the deceased. This man had to carry out the death sentence in the case of murder, or, in the case of accidental manslaughter, ensure that the guilty party remained in the city of refuge. Even in the case of manslaughter, blood had been shed. The person who had done this was not always completely free of guilt, even if it was just carelessness. He did not have to pay with his life if he moved to a city of refuge. There, he had to await the death of the high priest, whose own death would work the necessary atonement to enable him to return to his own land. It must also be said, however, that the requirement that a person guilty of manslaughter live in a separate Levitical city, away from his own village, lessened the temptation of the victim's family to take unlawful vengeance upon him. This factor must also have contributed to the formulation of this punishment.

We ought to note that the blood-redeemer was not free to choose to let a murderer off the hook. He received a task from God to avenge the spilling of blood. Only by executing the death penalty – after a judicial process – could the anger of God be appeased. The blood-redeemer was not to go hunting after a murderer on his own. He had to await the outcome of the judicial inquiry conducted by the elders of the region where the murder had occurred (Deut. 19). They would hand over the guilty party for execution. He could, of course, organise a search for someone suspected of the crime in order to put him on trial as the accused. But he was not to single-handedly try or execute anyone. In this respect the hypothetical case presented to king David in 2 Samuel 14:1-11 is interesting. The case is presented as follows (5b-7, 11):

---

58. On the principles of rendering justice in God's law, see the introduction and Anderson².

> "Alas, I am a widow; my husband is dead. [6] And your servant had two sons, and they quarreled with one another in the field. There was no one to separate them, and one struck the other and killed him. [7] And now the whole clan has risen against your servant, and they say, 'Give up the man who struck his brother, that we may put him to death for the life of his brother whom he killed.' And so they would destroy the heir also. Thus they would quench my coal that is left and leave to my husband neither name nor remnant on the face of the earth." ... [11] ... "Please let the king invoke the LORD your God, that the avenger of blood kill no more, and my son be not destroyed."

King David weighs up the importance of an heir to preserve the family inheritance in the Holy land over against the demand for the death penalty and promises that the guilty son will not be harmed. Joab, who had induced the woman to bring this hypothetical case, obviously perceived that this was the legal decision which David was likely to make. It shows that even the law demanding the death penalty for murder could, in extenuating circumstances, be overruled.

Finally, we ought not to think that the idea that murder desecrates the land is purely an Old Testament concept. In Revelation 6:10 we read of those who had been martyred for the faith. Their souls cry out to the Lord in prayer from under the heavenly altar ...

> "O Sovereign Lord, holy and true, how long before you will judge and avenge our blood on those who dwell on the earth?"

The blood of murder still cries to the Lord for (judicial) vengeance. This is something that we may — and even must — pray to God for. In modern Western society with its countless abortions, the church ought regularly to implore God to avenge the spilt blood in the land. We ought not to be afraid to sing prayers in the psalms crying out to the 'God of vengeance' (e.g. Ps. 94).

Parent-child crimes

It is evident from the penalties attached to assault on parents, kidnapping or declaring one's father or mother to be cursed[59] that God takes these matters very seriously (cf. Lev. 20:9; Deut. 27:16). In none of the three cases is the regular principle of restitution and punishment via *lex talionis* (the principle of 'eye for eye') applied. It is simply set aside in the case of assault on parents or kidnapping and inapplicable in a case referring to the use of words ('declaration of accursedness'). In fact slander or declaring others cursed, including judges and rulers, does not normally warrant civil punishment. For this reason such cursing is only prohibited in the second section of the book of the covenant, that without penal sanctions (Exod. 22:28).[60]

All three cases refer to the parent-child relationship. A kidnapper is presumed to be kidnapping a person to sell off as a slave. This would normally entail the kidnapping of a child.[61] It should be noted, however, that none of these laws restricts the crime to those children living at home. The laws against striking or declaring cursed speak equally to those children who would abuse ageing parents, whom they would be expected to care for.

Kidnapping

The law against kidnapping is repeated with small variations in Deuteronomy 24:7. Both laws describe a situation wherein someone is kidnapped and go on to give two possibilities.[62] Whether the kidnapped person has been sold off, or whether he is still in his possession, the

---

59. The Hebrew verb used (קלל *Piel*) does not mean 'to curse', but 'to declare to be cursed'.
60. As mentioned in the introduction, אֱלֹהִים in Exod. 22:28 refers to the 'gods', i.e. 'judges'. Cursing *God* himself is a capital offence, cf. Lev. 24:11-15.
61. Many translations misleadingly speak of kidnapping a 'man'. The Hebrew word (אִישׁ) here is merely used as an indefinite pronoun 'a person' / 'anyone'. In modern Western society we usually expect the motive for kidnapping to be ransom or perhaps the sex trade, forgetting that in ancient society nearly all kidnapping was for sale as slave.
62. See the textual commentary to v.16.

penalty remains the same, namely death.[63] The fact that this law is wedged between two laws specifically dealing with crimes against parents strongly suggests that kidnapping too is treated seriously because of the violation of the parent-child relationship when a child is stolen. In the case of a fellow Hebrew, there is the consideration that he may be sold out of the covenant community. More fundamental is perhaps the idea that autonomously taking control of a (once) free man encroaches upon a territory reserved for God alone. In addition, the loss of the child to parents also means the loss of a person who would have been responsible to care for them in sickness or old age. And we should not forget that the kidnapping of a covenant child would at the same time also be the kidnapping of an *heir* to the promised land. Of interest is the fact that kidnapping is also mentioned in a list of sins following the order of the fifth to the ninth commandments in 1 Timothy 1:10, where it takes the place of the eighth commandment (stealing).

Deuteronomy 24:7 restricts the law to the kidnapping of a fellow Hebrew. This raises the question as to whether Exodus 21 only intends to speak of kidnapping a fellow Hebrew, or whether the kidnapping of *anyone* would warrant the death penalty. Given the general principle that the same law must apply to the Israelite as to the foreigner (cf. for example, Lev. 24:22), it would seem that Exodus 21 intends the death penalty for kidnapping a person of any ethnicity. The restriction in Deuteronomy 24 must therefore be considered, not as a *limitation* of the law, but a specific warning against kidnapping a fellow Israelite. The tribes of Israel would be well aware that such kidnapping sadly belonged to their own history (cf. Gen. 37:25-28; 40:15). Only Joseph's mercy towards his brothers spared their lives. The Joseph tribes (Ephraim and Manasseh) could justly claim their double portion within the tribal structure of Israel (an application of the principle of *talio*, that is, 'eye for eye ...').

---

63. The verb in Deuteronomy translated 'mistreats' (NKJV) or 'treats him as a slave' (ESV) is only used twice, Deut. 24:7 and in Deut. 21:14. These translations are based on the interpretation of the Septuagint (which renders עמר Hithpael with καταδυναστεύω). *HAL* gives the meaning 'to trade' (based on comparative philology).

Declaring parents accursed

With respect to the case of a person declaring his parents to be cursed, we might note that this law (unlike Exod. 22:28) uses the *Piel participle* and not a finite verb form. The *Piel* participle implies habitual action.[64] The law is thus not referring to a child who in a fit of emotion suddenly and *uncharacteristically* declares his parents to be cursed, but one who has made such a declaration and lives accordingly. Such a declaration is in essence a prayer to God to rain down curses upon one's parents instead of blessings. In the expectation of such curses, such a child would naturally disassociate with his parents, having nothing to do with them. They are essentially disowned.

As stated above, violation of the parent relation is therefore set apart in all three cases. There is a special relationship with one's parents which makes these crimes the more heinous. The death penalty is, for example, not prescribed for assaulting or cursing one's neighbour. These sanctions relating to the abuse of parents are also much harsher than the penalties prescribed for similar offences in the surrounding nations, where it was common to have one's hand chopped off for striking one's parents.[65] The same point is made, somewhat more poetically, in Proverbs 20:20:

> *If one curses* (lit. 'declares to be accursed') *his father or his mother, his lamp will be put out in utter darkness.*

The Lord Jesus confirms the death penalty for this violation of the parent relation in Matthew 15:3-4 ...

> *He answered them, "And why do you break the commandment of God for the sake of your tradition? For God commanded, 'Honor your father and your mother,' and, 'Whoever reviles father or mother must surely die.'*

Why such a harsh penalty? There are a number of reasons why the relation with our parents is so important in the eyes of God. Firstly,

---

64. See Jenni², 77-87 and esp. 84.
65. See, for example, the *codex Hammurabi* § 195 which only applies punishment when the father is struck. This law code also uses the *lex talionis* for assaults on one's neighbour, but applies the principle of the removal of the offending body part to specific cases of familial assault.

our parents are the people who brought us into being – under God's blessing. In giving us life they were obeying the command of God to fill the earth and rule over it. Our origin lies with them. That life-giving relationship is very special. A number of God's laws stress the importance of this relationship. Take, for example, the mysterious rule (Exod. 23:19b):

> You shall not boil a young goat in its mother's milk.

By boiling a kid in the milk of its mother the holy relationship between mother and child is defiled – the relationship between child and the one that gave that child life. Children all too often do not appreciate the difficulty their parents went through in order to bring them into the world, to rear and educate them, not to speak of the pain in childbirth.

But there is also a second reason why this relationship is very special. God gave us as children to our parents. We were entrusted to them. Fathers and mothers must rear their children in the fear of the LORD (cf. Deut. 4:9-10). They promise this when they baptise them. God is our heavenly Father and he gives our fathers and mothers the task of bringing us up in his holy name. God is thus the being who stands behind our parents in their raising of us.

Declaring one's father or mother to be cursed is not the only violation of the parent/child relationship which can bring a death penalty upon a child. Striking them is equally serious. Assault on one's parents is tantamount to assault on God himself.

A concrete example of someone who deserves the death penalty for despising his parents is given in Deuteronomy 21:18-21.

> *[18] If a man has a stubborn and rebellious son who will not obey the voice of his father or the voice of his mother, and, though they discipline him, will not listen to them, [19] then his father and his mother shall take hold of him and bring him out to the elders of his city at the gate of the place where he lives, [20] and they shall say to the elders of his city, 'This our son is stubborn and rebellious; he will not obey our voice; he is a glutton and a drunkard.' [21] Then all the men of the city shall stone him to death with stones. So you*

shall purge the evil from your midst, and all Israel shall hear, and fear.

It is good that this case-law provides us with such a clear example so that we do not misunderstand God's intention and think that little children who might from time to time say a bad word against their parents or hit them in a temper tantrum should be put to death. Deuteronomy 21 shows us a son who can no longer be held under control by his parents. He is a drunk and a 'glutton', perhaps better translated 'contemptuous'.[66] He is stubborn and rebellious. What is more, this fact is assumed to be well-known. The men of the city are to engage in the stoning. In God's law the *witnesses* to a crime are those who must throw the first stones (Deut. 17:6-7), and in this case the witnesses are clearly the men of the city, not the parents. The parents are the ones who must judge the situation so serious that they bring their son for prosecution. It is an extreme remedy meant for cases where no other discipline will work. The parents must bear witness that they have done their best to discipline their child – all to no avail. Such a child must be removed from the people. Continued uncontrollable rebelliousness cannot be tolerated.

As noted above, the Lord Jesus cites this law in his discussion with the Pharisees. He places the law concerning someone who has declared his parents accursed next to the fifth commandment requiring honour to parents. He shows thereby that declaring someone to be accursed is the opposite of honouring. In the Hebrew language 'to honour' literally means 'to give weight to'. Over against this, 'to declare cursed' means literally 'to make light'. Such a declaration indicates a loathing of one's parents. Jesus shows that this commandment applies equally, if not more, to adult children. Scope for aggression against aged parents was all the more present in a society where the aged were often completely dependant upon their children for care, especially if they became weak, sick or senile. This consideration also highlights

---

66. The word זוֹלֵל is not common, but the root goes back to the same origin as דלל. The translation 'glutton' relies on the context of its use here and in Prov. 32:21 and 28:7. Both *HAL* as well as Baumann's article (215) suggest a meaning such as 'rash' or 'contemptuous'.

another problem when a child is kidnapped. The social security for parents has been stolen.

Text

| ¹² Ἐὰν δὲ πατάξῃ τίς τινα, καὶ ἀποθάνῃ, θανάτῳ θανατούσθω· ¹³ ὁ δὲ οὐχ ἑκών, ἀλλὰ ὁ θεὸς παρέδωκεν εἰς τὰς χεῖρας αὐτοῦ, δώσω σοι τόπον, οὗ φεύξεται ἐκεῖ ὁ φονεύσας. ¹⁴ Ἐὰν δέ τις ἐπιθῆται τῷ πλησίον ἀποκτεῖναι αὐτὸν δόλῳ, καὶ καταφύγῃ, ἀπὸ τοῦ θυσιαστηρίου μου λήμψῃ αὐτὸν θανατῶσαι. ¹⁵ Ὃς τύπτει πατέρα αὐτοῦ ἢ μητέρα αὐτοῦ, θανάτῳ θανατούσθω. ¹⁶ ὁ κακολογῶν πατέρα αὐτοῦ ἢ μητέρα αὐτοῦ θανάτῳ τελευτάτω. ¹⁷ Ὃς ἐὰν κλέψῃ τίς τινα τῶν υἱῶν Ἰσραήλ, καὶ καταδυναστεύσας αὐτὸν ἀποδῶται, καὶ εὑρεθῇ ἐν αὐτῷ, θανάτῳ τελευτάτω. | מַכֵּה אִישׁ וָמֵת מוֹת יוּמָת: ¹³ וַאֲשֶׁר לֹא צָדָה וְהָאֱלֹהִים אִנָּה לְיָדוֹ וְשַׂמְתִּי לְךָ מָקוֹם אֲשֶׁר יָנוּס שָׁמָּה: ¹⁴ וְכִי־יָזִד אִישׁ עַל־רֵעֵהוּ לְהָרְגוֹ בְעָרְמָה מֵעִם מִזְבְּחִי תִּקָּחֶנּוּ לָמוּת: ¹⁵ וּמַכֵּה אָבִיו וְאִמּוֹ מוֹת יוּמָת: ¹⁶ וְגֹנֵב אִישׁ וּמְכָרוֹ וְנִמְצָא בְיָדוֹ מוֹת יוּמָת: ¹⁷ וּמְקַלֵּל אָבִיו וְאִמּוֹ מוֹת יוּמָת: |

צדה, *Qal* to lie in wait	עָרְמָה, cleverness, cunning
אנה, *Piel* to cause to happen	καταδυναστεύω, to oppress
יזד, *Hiph.* to become hot	

21:12

מַכֵּה אִישׁ וָמֵת / Ἐὰν δὲ πατάξῃ τίς

'A striker of a man and he (the man) dies'. This grammatical construction, while not possible in Greek (or English) is not unknown in Hebrew, cf. Jouön/Muraoka §119r. On the question of a copulative, see the note to 21:4.

וָמֵת

Instead of the expected וּמֵת we have a 'strong vocalisation', used before monosyllabic words to provide strong stress, cf. Jouön/Muraoka §104d. It occurs here as the last word of the protasis (contrast v.20).

מוֹת יוּמָת

The syntax is very compact. We might have expected the resumptive pronoun הוּא. Note that the use of the absolute infinitive as internal accusative adds emphasis, but does not determine the mood of the finite verb. The mood is determined by the context. Theoretically the phrase could mean "he must surely be killed", "he may surely be killed" or "he should surely be killed". Although the infinitive absolute is usually the same conjugation as the verb, the *Qal* may also serve for all conjugations as here, cf. Jouön/Muraoka §123p.

21:13

לְיָדוֹ / εἰς τὰς χεῖρας αὐτοῦ

The LXX read לידיו. There is also a Qumran ms with this reading in Hebrew.

וְשַׂמְתִּי / δώσω

This is the so-called '*waw* of apodosis'. Note that it is absent in the previous verse because it is not used when the apodosis does not begin with a verb (the infin. absl. is considered to be a noun), cf. Jouön/ Muraoka §176d, m. It is not reflected in the LXX and would not be idiomatic in Greek.

ὁ φονεύσας

The LXX adds the equivalent of הָרֹצֵחַ, cf. Num. 35:6.

21:14

יָזִד / ἐπιθῆται

The verb ἐπιτίθημαι + infin. refers to making an attempt to do something (i.e. putting one's hand to something). Possibly the LXX read יָעַז (to attack).

מֵעִם מִזְבְּחִי / καὶ καταφύγῃ, ἀπὸ τοῦ θυσιαστηρίου μου

The LXX adds the equivalent of וְנָס מִמִּזְבָּחִי.

לָמוּת / θανατῶσαι
   The LXX appears to have read לְהָמִית.

21:15

וּמַכֵּה

The word-order of the following verses indicates 'circumstantial' clauses connecting these laws together in one combined section.

אָבִיו וְאִמּוֹ

These definite direct objects lack the object marker אֶת־ and are thus not individuated. The same phenomenon is found in v.17. This is probably stylistic, following the substantive participle and mirroring the syntax of v.12.

21:16

For the grammar of this verse see the comment on v.12. It is interesting to note that the LXX has transposed vs. 15 and 17, both of which deal with assault to parents.

τινα τῶν υἱῶν Ισραηλ καὶ καταδυναστεύσας αὐτὸν

The LXX rendering of the verse on kidnapping is significantly longer. It specifies the victim as one of the sons of Israel who is abused and then sold. The text reflects a conflation of the law in Exodus with that in Deut. 24:7, reading מִבְּנֵי יִשְׂרָאֵל וְהִתְעַמֶּר־בּוֹ after אִישׁ.

וּמְכָרוֹ וְנִמְצָא / ἀποδῶται, καὶ εὑρεθῇ

Two possibilities are presented, i.e. the *waws* should be interpreted as 'either … or', cf. Jouön/Muraoka §175ab. As far as the LXX is concerned, note that the middle voice of δίδωμι is typically used of selling.

21:17

וּמְקַלֵּל

On words for cursing, see the textual note to 22:27 (Eng. v.28).

21:18-19

Assault against a freeman

Translation

¹⁸ And when men contend and one strikes the other with a stone or with his fist and he does not die but he collapses to his bed,

¹⁹ if he arises and walks about outside leaning on a walking stick, then it happens that the man who struck him becomes blameless. He should only pay for his inactivity and surely bring about healing.

Commentary

As we have seen above, if a free man (or woman) dies as a result of an assault, God's law counts this as murder and the death penalty is mandatory. The case in verses 18-19 is different. Not only is there assault which does not lead to death, the assault in question is the result of two persons quarrelling, both evidently using violence. Such fighting seems to have been not uncommon (cf. Exod. 2:13; Lev. 24:10; Isa. 58:4). God's law does not require the judges to ascertain who started the fight and who was right in terms of the quarrel. If someone is injured, the other party must pay for his loss of time (e.g. reparation for lost business, or the costs of another to work in his stead) and for his medical expenses. In other words, there must be reparation for damages, but there is no penalty as such. Those who engage in fighting ought to expect to take the consequences. Damage done while fighting is thus not considered to be accidental, but neither is it considered to be a normal kind of assault. This is due to the fact that both men were attacking each other. An assault without cause (i.e. where only one party engages in violence) would involve both reparation and a penalty based on the principle of the *lex talionis* (see below). The Lord Jesus warns against engaging in violence and teaches us to turn the other cheek when violence is used against us by evil individuals (Matt. 5:39).

Text

¹⁸ Ἐὰν δὲ λοιδορῶνται δύο ἄνδρες, καὶ πατάξῃ τις τὸν πλησίον λίθῳ ἢ πυγμῇ, καὶ μὴ ἀποθάνῃ, κατακλιθῇ δὲ ἐπὶ τὴν κοίτην, ¹⁹ ἐὰν ἐξαναστὰς ὁ ἄνθρωπος περιπατήσῃ ἔξω ἐπὶ ῥάβδου, ἀθῷος ἔσται ὁ πατάξας· πλὴν τῆς ἀργίας αὐτοῦ ἀποτείσει καὶ τὰ ἰατρεῖα.	וְכִי־יְרִיבֻן אֲנָשִׁים וְהִכָּה־אִישׁ אֶת־רֵעֵהוּ בְּאֶבֶן אוֹ בְאֶגְרֹף וְלֹא יָמוּת וְנָפַל לְמִשְׁכָּב: ¹⁹ אִם־יָקוּם וְהִתְהַלֵּךְ בַּחוּץ עַל־מִשְׁעַנְתּוֹ וְנִקָּה הַמַּכֶּה רַק שִׁבְתּוֹ יִתֵּן וְרַפֹּא יְרַפֵּא:
אֶגְרֹף, fist	מִשְׁעֶנֶת, support, staff

21:18

יְרִיבֻן / λοιδορῶνται

Although the Hebrew term is often used in a legal context, it can also (as here) designate a common quarrelling. The Greek denotes slandering or reviling. The *paragogic nun* added to imperfect forms ending in ו is an archaism. It is regular in the spelling of cognate languages such as Ugaritic, Arabic and Aramaic. It is rare in late Biblical Hebrew or early rabbinic Hebrew, see further Jouön/Muraoka §44e.

אֲנָשִׁים / δύο ἄνδρες

Is the LXX interpreting the situation or did the translator interpret the vowels as a dual (אֲנָשַׁיִם)?

21:19

וְנִקָּה הַמַּכֶּה

Although the verb could be theoretically construed either as *Piel* or *Niphal*, in context it can only be *Niphal*. The *Piel* is declarative/estimative 'to declare to be free from punishment' often with the nuance that therefore someone can be left unpunished. The basic meaning of the root is 'to be נָקִי (blameless)'. This gives for the *Niphal* the ingressive (becoming) causative middle of causing the transition into the state of being blameless. The subject is here not the *controller* of the activity and so we must paraphrase: 'then it happens that the man (who struck) becomes blameless'. It is interesting to note that the verb נקה is not used in the *Qal* (except for the absl. infin. together with a finite verb in the *Niphal*). Jenni[4] (259) suggests that the preponderance of the *Niphal* and lack of the use of the *Qal* are due to the fact that being 'blameless' is not a concrete property, but one that needs to be declared by a higher authority (usually God). The *result* is then rendered in the *Niphal*. The actual declaration of blamelessness is not stipulated in our text, but assumed.

שִׁבְתּוֹ

The verbal noun שֶׁבֶת could be interpreted either as a derivative of שׁבת ('to cease / rest') or of ישׁב ('to sit'). In either case the point is that the perpetrator must pay for his forced inactivity. Note the omission of אֶת־, which is common when the direct object precedes the verb.

וְרַפֹּא יְרַפֵּא

'Then he will certainly bring about healing'. The *Piel* emphasises the result and does not indicate who it is that actually brings the result about, cf. Jenni[2], 144.

21:20-21

Assault against a slave

Translation

[20] And when a man strikes his male slave or his married slave-woman with his rod and the slave dies under his hand, then he must certainly be avenged.

[21] Only if after a day or two he stands up will he not be avenged for he is his (master's) asset[67].

Commentary

A slave does not have the same rights as a free man. Technically, a slave is the property of his master (in a similar way to which children belong to their parents). The master is therefore responsible for his food and shelter. Slaves have no real motivation to work except through the threat of discipline and the master has the right to exercise corporal punishment on his slaves in the same way that he might discipline his children (cf. Prov. 10:13; 13:24; 22:15; 23:13-14; 29:15). The Hebrew speaks literally of 'the rod', implying that a rod belongs to the master's normal equipment.[68] This law (and that of 21:26-27) seeks to place limitations on the effects of such punishment and to punish its abuse.

It should be noted that the law mentions a male slave or a married female slave (*'āmāh*). It would be highly unusual for an unmarried female slave (*shiphchāh*) to be in the service of a male master, for they were normally restricted in service to the lady of the house.

---

67. *Lit.* 'money'.
68. Houtman, *ad loc.*

If a slave dies as a result of his beating, the death of the slave must be 'avenged' upon his master.[69] Although not explicit, the text clearly implies the death penalty for the master.[70] The law is elsewhere explicit that all murder requires the death penalty (see above). If another punishment had been intended this would need to be spelled out. Jewish traditions (Samaritan Pentateuch, Targums) also argue explicitly for the death penalty.[71] Indeed Chirichigno has argued that this unusual legal expression expressing the need for vengeance against the crime, suggests that if there are no witnesses God himself will execute the judgment.[72]

On one popular rendering of verse 21 (e.g. the Septuagint and several modern translations) the law proceeds to give the master the benefit of the doubt if the slave is able to stand and dies a day or two later.[73] On this interpretation the verb 'to stand' (עמד) is interpreted in terms of 'surviving'. The reasoning is then that the slave may have died from other causes. This interpretation seems rather weak. If he dies a day or two later after having been severely beaten, we should at least speak of manslaughter. The problem is, however, that Numbers 35 shows that God's law interprets manslaughter (death resulting from intent to harm) as murder. The death penalty should still be applied. There is, however, another possible interpretation. In Hebrew (just as with Greek ἵστημι) the verb 'to stand' can indicate standing up after having been in a position of lying or sitting. This is well illustrated by Nehemiah 8:5 where we are told that the congregation 'stood up' (עמד) when Ezra opened the scroll of the law. On this interpretation verse 21 is saying that if the beaten slave recovers from his bed after one or two days, the master is not to be avenged. After all, the slave is his asset (lit. 'money'). He has injured his own possession and punished himself by putting the slave out of action for several days. In addition, since the

---

69. So also the ESV. The NASB and NKJV incorrectly read 'punished'.
70. This is made explicit in the Sam. Pent., which reads "he must certainly be killed" (מות יומת) for "he must certainly be avenged".
71. Despite all this there are still some modern commentators who suggest that a lighter punishment was intended.
72. Chirichigno, 163-69.
73. The NASB/ESV follow the LXX rendering 'survives'. Literally the text reads: 'stands', which is then interpreted as 'still able to stand'.

slave is his possession, the master is self-evidently responsible for his medical treatment. On this interpretation there is also a direct parallel with the previous law (v.19).[74]

Some commentators have argued that this law only applies to foreign slaves, citing Leviticus 25:44-46 (cf. vs.43 and 53) where God says that Hebrew slaves are not to be ruled over with severity. In context, however, Leviticus may be referring to limitations placed on the length of slavery for Hebrews and the fact that Hebrew slaves cannot be passed on through inheritance. Even *if* there is a reference to the kind of toil to which they may be subjected, this does not amount to a prohibition against disciplining them. The text in Exodus contains no hint that only a certain kind of slave is in view here.

Text

| ²⁰ Ἐὰν δέ τις πατάξῃ τὸν παῖδα αὐτοῦ ἢ τὴν παιδίσκην αὐτοῦ ἐν ῥάβδῳ, καὶ ἀποθάνῃ ὑπὸ τὰς χεῖρας αὐτοῦ, δίκῃ ἐκδικηθήτω. ²¹ ἐὰν δὲ διαβιώσῃ ἡμέραν μίαν ἢ δύο, οὐκ ἐκδικηθήσεται· τὸ γὰρ ἀργύριον αὐτοῦ ἐστιν. | 20 וְכִי־יַכֶּה אִישׁ אֶת־עַבְדּוֹ אוֹ אֶת־אֲמָתוֹ בַּשֵּׁבֶט וּמֵת תַּחַת יָדוֹ נָקֹם יִנָּקֵם׃ 21 אַךְ אִם־יוֹם אוֹ יוֹמַיִם יַעֲמֹד לֹא יֻקַּם כִּי כַסְפּוֹ הוּא׃ |

21:20

בַּשֵּׁבֶט

The use of the definite article defines a rod as part of the normal equipment of the master.

אֶת־אֲמָתוֹ

An אָמָה is a married female slave. An unmarried female slave (שִׁפְחָה) would not normally belong to a male owner.

---

74. In this I follow the exegesis of Chirichigno, 169-77.

תַּחַת יָדוֹ / ὑπὸ τὰς χεῖρας αὐτοῦ

The LXX has read יָדָיו, which may imply that the master somewhat viciously used both hands to wield his rod in beating the slave to death.

נָקֹם יִנָּקֵם

Despite the *Niphal* finite verb, a *Qal* infinitive absolute (instead of *Niphal*) is often used for emphasis. Note that נקם is an *accomplishment* verb (i.e. denoting both the process or action and its result) and therefore the *Qal* can be interpreted as causative: 'to cause vengeance to take place'. For this reason *accomplishment* verbs in the *Qal* do not have a *Hiphil* conjugation, given that the *Qal* is already causative (and indeed there is no *Hiphil* form for נקם). The *Niphal*, which normally functions as the middle conjugation of the ingressive *Hiphil*, in such a situation takes its meaning from the *Qal*. The *Niphal* is then: 'to let vengeance happen with respect to oneself' which may be interpreted either actively or passively according to context. Here the sense is obviously passive (although it is the only example of a medio-passive *Niphal* for this verb): 'he must certainly be avenged'.[75]

21:21

יַעֲמֹד / διαβιώσῃ

The interpretation of the LXX ('to survive') has been influential for the understanding of this verse. There is, however, another way of understanding this verb ('to stand'), namely the action of standing up from a position of lying or sitting (cf. Neh. 8:5). See the main commentary for a discussion on how this can radically change the interpretation.

יֻקָּם

There are three instances of נקם which are sometimes referred to as *Hophal* (Gen. 4:15, 24; Exod. 21:21). The fact that *accomplishment* verbs in the *Qal* do not have a *Hiphil* conjugation casts severe doubts on this interpretation, for which reason they are regularly regarded as *Qal* passive forms (which have the same spelling).

---

75. For this explanation in general see Jenni⁴, specifically concerning נקם on pp.203-206.

21:22-25

Unintentional assault on a pregnant woman and the lex talionis

Translation

[22] And when men fight and they hit a pregnant woman and her offspring comes out[76] and there is no harm, a fine shall surely be imposed according as the husband[77] of the woman places upon him and he will pay according to the assessing judges.

[23] And if harm occurs, then you shall pay life for life,

[24] eye for eye, tooth for tooth, hand for hand, foot for foot,

[25] burn for burn, wound for wound, slash for slash.

Commentary

This law concerns fighting men who cause accidental injury to a pregnant woman. It is important to understand the legal background to the judgment given in this law. In the first place accidental injury to a person would normally not require any restitution. However, when injury is caused by such irresponsible behaviour as fighting, the injury can clearly be attributed to negligence so that restitution would be required (e.g. payment for loss of earnings and medical expenses, cf. 21:19). It is with these principles as a point of departure that we need to consider this law. It concerns the special case of accidental injury

---

76. The Massoretic Text reads the plural 'children', which may be a plural of generalisation. The LXX and Sam. Pent. render 'child'.
77. The Hebrew word for 'husband' literally means 'master', although it is a different word to 'master' in the sense of owner (e.g. the master/owner of a slave).

by fighting men to a pregnant woman. The respect due to a pregnant woman means that fighting men, who come too near her or who may be confronted with a pregnant woman that tries to break up the fight (cf. Deut. 25:11; 2 Sam. 14:6) will be subject to the *lex talionis* ('eye for eye' etc.) for a penalty payment. That is to say, the case is treated the same as if they intentionally set out to harm the woman.

Crucial to a correct understanding of this law is the interpretation of the nature of the damage done to the child in the woman's womb. Is she said to experience a miscarriage or a premature birth?

The Greek Septuagint translation interprets the Hebrew phrase of verse 22 translated here "and there is no harm" as "not completely formed".[78] A complete translation of the Septuagint reads:

> *If two men fight and strike a pregnant woman and her child comes out and it is not fully formed, he will surely be fined, according as the woman's husband demands he will give (in accordance) with the assessment. But if it was fully formed he will give life for life...*

It is unclear to me whether the Septuagint translators were guessing as to the meaning of the operative word *'asōn*, or whether they possibly read another text. Wevers suggests that the translators interpreted the word in terms of a more (hypothetical) literal meaning of 'health', i.e. "and it was not healthy" (therefore, 'not fully formed').[79] In any case, the point is that if the foetus was not fully formed, it would be difficult to literally apply the *lex talionis* because the body parts may not be able to be appropriately distinguished. For this reason a fine is imposed in the case of an unformed foetus. There would appear to be a large measure of theorising here on the part of the translators, without much practical experience. In addition, it is unclear whether the translators expected an unformed foetus to be still alive. In any case, the possibility that a formed foetus remained alive is certain, because of the application of the *lex talionis* (i.e. the idea that a living child might have one or other damaged limb). The first century AD –

---

78. The phrases are respectively ולא יהיה אסון and μὴ ἐξεικονισμένον.
79. Wevers, 333-34. This interpretation presumes that the translators saw a relationship to Aramaic אסי (to be strong, well).

BC Alexandrian Jew Philo interpreted the Septuagint here as referring to a premature birth in both cases.[80]

If the text refers to a miscarriage,[81] then the point of the *lex talionis* refers to further injury to the mother. The monetary fine demanded by her husband is in lieu of losing the life of his child (one could hardly speak of 'child for child' in such a case). On this interpretation the death of the unborn child is not treated as murder or as manslaughter, but as a form of injury.

If the text refers to a premature birth, then the *lex talionis* refers to any further injury done to either the child or the mother and the monetary fine (which we would expect to be considerably less than in the first interpretation) is for the discomfort afforded the mother.

The text itself only says that the child 'comes out,' not that it is dead. Given the respect shown in the rest of the Old Testament for life from the moment of conception which is formed by God (cf. Job 31:15; Ps. 51:5; 139:13-16; Jer. 1:5), the most obvious reading must be a reference to premature birth. This interpretation also makes sense of the phrase "he will pay according to the assessing judges".[82] In the case of the *lex talionis* the judges normally mediate, but do not determine the fine, which is a result of the negotiation between the victim and perpetrator(s). That the judges must here determine the fine follows from the judgment that the pregnant woman has been hit resulting in a premature birth, but there is no further harm to mother or child. There is, therefore, no basis for a negotiation based on the *lex talionis*.

As stated above, further damage to either child or mother is to be punished according to the principle of 'like for like'. This is the principle used when injury is sustained with intent to harm and is

---

80. *Cong.* 137-38.
81. As, for example, Josephus, *Ant.* 4.278 interpreted it.
82. The translation "as the judges determine" is the traditional interpretation of the phrase בִּפְלִלִים (only used here), which goes right back to the interpretation of the Aramaic Targums. The LXX reads μετὰ ἀξιώματος ('with the assessment'). Scholars who argue that this law concerns a miscarriage and that the payment to the husband is an application of the *lex talionis* for the aborted child have a vested interest in arguing that this traditional interpretation is incorrect.

applied here when fighting men cause injury to a pregnant woman. There is good reason to believe, however, that the principle was generally only literally applied in the case of death. God specifically forbade the principle of 'life for life' in the case of murder to be commuted to a fine (Num. 35:31). But the principle 'eye for eye, tooth for tooth, etc.' was a legal principle stating the need for a punishment equal to the crime. See further the discussion of this principle in the introduction.[83]

---

83. It is interesting to note that the *lex talionis* (which as a principle was common to all ancient cultures) appears in a very similar formulation in the *codex Hammurabi* (§§ 196, 197, 200): "If a man has destroyed the sight of another similar person, they shall destroy his sight. If he has broken another man's bone, they shall break one of his bones. ... (200) If a man has knocked out the tooth of a man who is his colleague, they shall knock out his tooth". (transl. Richardson). The principle is quite differently applied however. In the first place, it is only applicable to freedmen, not to slaves or others who are in subjection. Secondly, the financial equivalents which can be sought are specified and not left to a bargaining process between the plaintiff and the perpetrator. In addition, the principle is sometimes even applied in respect of the persons belonging to the perpetrator's household (e.g. if someone strikes and kills the daughter of a citizen, the perpetrator's daughter must be killed! §§ 209-10).

Text

²² Ἐὰν δὲ μάχωνται δύο ἄνδρες καὶ πατάξωσιν γυναῖκα ἐν γαστρὶ ἔχουσαν, καὶ ἐξέλθῃ τὸ παιδίον αὐτῆς μὴ ἐξεικονισμένον, ἐπιζήμιον ζημιωθήσεται· καθότι ἂν ἐπιβάλῃ ὁ ἀνὴρ τῆς γυναικός, δώσει μετὰ ἀξιώματος· ²³ ἐὰν δὲ ἐξεικονισμένον ᾖ, δώσει ψυχὴν ἀντὶ ψυχῆς, ²⁴ ὀφθαλμὸν ἀντὶ ὀφθαλμοῦ, ὀδόντα ἀντὶ ὀδόντος, χεῖρα ἀντὶ χειρός, πόδα ἀντὶ ποδός, ²⁵ κατάκαυμα ἀντὶ κατακαύματος, τραῦμα ἀντὶ τραύματος, μώλωπα ἀντὶ μώλωπος.	וְכִי־יִנָּצוּ אֲנָשִׁים וְנָגְפוּ אִשָּׁה הָרָה וְיָצְאוּ יְלָדֶיהָ וְלֹא יִהְיֶה אָסוֹן עָנוֹשׁ יֵעָנֵשׁ כַּאֲשֶׁר יָשִׁית עָלָיו בַּעַל הָאִשָּׁה וְנָתַן בִּפְלִלִים: ²³ וְאִם־אָסוֹן יִהְיֶה וְנָתַתָּה נֶפֶשׁ תַּחַת נָפֶשׁ: ²⁴ עַיִן תַּחַת עַיִן שֵׁן תַּחַת שֵׁן יָד תַּחַת יָד רֶגֶל תַּחַת רָגֶל: ²⁵ כְּוִיָּה תַּחַת כְּוִיָּה פֶּצַע תַּחַת פָּצַע חַבּוּרָה תַּחַת חַבּוּרָה:

נצה, *Niph.* to fight	שׁית, *Qal* to set, stand, place
נגף, *Qal* to injure by striking	כְּוִיָּה, burning, branding (only used here)
אָסוֹן, harm[84]	פֶּצַע, wound
ענשׁ, *Qal* to impose a fine	חַבּוּרָה, wound, slash

21:22

אֲנָשִׁים / δύο ἄνδρες

See the comment at 21:18.

וְיָצְאוּ יְלָדֶיהָ / καὶ ἐξέλθῃ τὸ παιδίον αὐτῆς

The LXX reads the singular verb and noun as does the Sam. Pent. (ויצא ולדה). Jouön/Muraoka §136j interprets the text as a plural of generalisation ('offspring').

---

84. *HAL* defines the word as 'fatal accident', but given the context and application of the *talio* this is impossible. *DCH* more appropriately gives the meaning 'harm'.

וְלֹא יִהְיֶה אָסוֹן / μὴ ἐξεικονισμένον

For comment on the LXX translation see the main commentary.

עָנוֹשׁ יֵעָנֵשׁ

See the comment at 21:20 in regard to נָקֹם יִנָּקֵם.

בִּפְלִלִים / μετὰ ἀξιώματος

The Hebrew noun is only found three times, here, in Deut. 32:31 ('our enemies are פְּלִילִים') and Job 31:11 ('iniquity of פְּלִילִים'). Traditionally the noun has been taken to mean 'judge' or 'assessor' based on the (rare) cognate verb פלל Piel to judge, arbitrate (*DCH* 'to assess'). Other views have been argued, but the main dictionaries have tended not to accept them. There remains a degree of uncertainty.[85] The LXX interprets 'with the assessment'.

21:23

וְנָתַתָּה נֶפֶשׁ תַּחַת נֶפֶשׁ / δώσει ψυχὴν ἀντὶ ψυχῆς

The LXX has read נָתַן. The spelling of the 2nd person singular of נתן with an added ה is quite common. Jouön/Muraoka (§42f) suggest that it may be 'a sort of compensation for the graphic abbreviation arising from the assimilation'. It is also common in *lamed-he* verbs.

---

85. Cf. Gerstenberger, 574.

21:26-27

Permanent damage to a slave by lashing out

Translation

²⁶ And when a man strikes the eye of his slave or the eye of his married slave-woman and ruins it, he shall set him free as recompense for his eye.

²⁷ And if it is the tooth of his slave or the tooth of his married slave-woman that he knocks out, he shall set him free as recompense for his tooth.

Commentary

This law follows immediately upon the mention of the *lex talionis* ('eye for eye ...') because it treats an exception to this legal principle. Slaves do not have the right to take their master to court and sue for damages done to their body. However, the law protects slaves in a way that is more far-reaching than a court settlement. It grants them their freedom from the tyranny of a cruel master. Any form of lasting physical injury exacted on the slave is punished by allowing him his freedom. Eyes and teeth are clearly intended as examples, but the mention of the face strongly suggests that the law is aimed at masters who have lashed out at their slaves. Regular punishment by means of the rod would have been meted out upon the person's back with no risk of hitting his face.

As with the law on an assault against a slave (21:20-21) only a male slave or a *married* female slave (*'āmāh*) is mentioned. It would be highly unusual for an unmarried female slave (*shiphchāh*) to be in the service of a male master, for they were normally restricted in service to the lady of the house.

Although it is not specifically stated here, if the slave is a Hebrew – that is, someone sold into slavery because of debt – his freedom not only means that the debt is repaid early, but, if he is a land-holder, his master is duty bound to supply him with animals, seed and wine so that he has the opportunity to make a living for himself (Deut. 15:12-15). It should be noted that debt-slavery did not force the debtor to sell himself to his creditor. He had the option of selling himself to whomever he chose so that the price of his six-year slave term could be paid to the creditor. If he made a bad choice and sold himself to a person who turned out to be a cruel master, a beating which ruined any body-part would be sufficient to allow him to go free. If the slave were a foreigner, he is set free from what otherwise would have been slavery for life. In this case, the master is not bound to supply him with animals or food, but the law does encourage support for the needy foreigner. It is possible that such a person could not support himself, but he would, at the very least, have the opportunity of selling himself to another master of his own choice.

As with the law in 21:20-21 we see here a further incentive to masters not to abuse their slaves when discipline is exercised. This law is not reflected in any of the other legal codes from the Ancient Near East, where masters had the right to harm their slaves as they wished. Job 31:13-15 warns the reader that God watches over the slave when he files a complaint against his master.

Text

²⁶ Ἐὰν δέ τις πατάξῃ τὸν ὀφθαλμὸν τοῦ οἰκέτου αὐτοῦ ἢ τὸν ὀφθαλμὸν τῆς θεραπαίνης αὐτοῦ, καὶ ἐκτυφλώσῃ, ἐλευθέρους ἐξαποστελεῖ αὐτοὺς ἀντὶ τοῦ ὀφθαλμοῦ αὐτῶν. ²⁷ Ἐὰν δὲ τὸν ὀδόντα τοῦ οἰκέτου ἢ τὸν ὀδόντα τῆς θεραπαίνης αὐτοῦ ἐκκόψῃ, ἐλευθέρους ἐξαποστελεῖ αὐτοὺς ἀντὶ τοῦ ὀδόντος αὐτῶν.	וְכִי־יַכֶּה אִישׁ אֶת־עֵין עַבְדּוֹ אוֹ־אֶת־עֵין אֲמָתוֹ וְשִׁחֲתָהּ לַחָפְשִׁי יְשַׁלְּחֶנּוּ תַּחַת עֵינוֹ: ²⁷ וְאִם־שֵׁן עַבְדּוֹ אוֹ־שֵׁן אֲמָתוֹ יַפִּיל לַחָפְשִׁי יְשַׁלְּחֶנּוּ תַּחַת שִׁנּוֹ:

21:26

עַבְדּוֹ ... אֲמָתוֹ / τοῦ οἰκέτου αὐτοῦ ... τῆς θεραπαίνης αὐτοῦ

In this law, the LXX distinguishes the slave terminology from Exod. 21:20-21, although the Hebrew terminology remains the same. The LXX makes a distinction between regular slaves considered to be working outside of the master's house (21:20-21) and domestic slaves, to which this law applies. The implication is that domestic slaves have more rights. Does this perhaps reflect the situation in Hellenistic times? There was certainly a cultural and social distinction made between the lower agricultural slaves and the higher status of domestic slaves. However, I am not aware of any legal distinction ever having been made between them.

וְשִׁחֲתָהּ / καὶ ἐκτυφλώσῃ

Wevers considers the Greek (transitive) verb to be used absolutely here and to imply complete blindness (i.e. affecting both eyes). This is not necessary. The implied object of the verb is the eye that has been struck.

יְשַׁלְּחֶנּוּ תַּחַת עֵינוֹ / ἐξαποστελεῖ αὐτοὺς ἀντὶ τοῦ ὀφθαλμοῦ αὐτῶν

In both verses the LXX uses plural suffixes for the singular suffixes of MT.

21:27

וְאִם־שֵׁן עַבְדּוֹ אוֹ־שֵׁן אֲמָתוֹ

The fronted teeth are not individuated by אֶת־, which is common when a direct object precedes its verb. On the question whether this fronting should be considered an example of emphasis, see the note at 21:31.

21:28-32

CASE LAWS
LAWS WITH PENAL SANCTIONS:
3. LAWS INVOLVING ANIMALS

Laws concerning a goring head of cattle

Translation

[28] And when a head of cattle gores a man or a woman and he dies, then the animal must be stoned and its flesh may not be eaten, but the owner of the animal will be deemed innocent.

[29] But if a head of cattle was previously[86] prone to goring and witness (of this) has been borne to its owner and he has not confined[87] it and it kills a man or a woman, then the animal shall be stoned and also its owner shall be killed.

[30] If a ransom price is laid upon him then he shall render the redemption price for his life according to everything which is laid upon him.

[31] Whether it gores a son or it gores a daughter, he shall be dealt with according to this judgement.

[32] If the head of cattle gores a slave or a married female slave, then he shall pay 30 shekels to his owner and the animal shall be stoned.

---

86. *Lit.* "from yesterday and the day before" – an idiom for 'previously'.
87. LXX 'destroyed'.

Commentary

The use of domestic cattle

The Israelites left Egypt with great numbers of livestock (Exod. 12:38), a blessing of God which, however, did require regulation. This law addresses the question of death caused by a domestic animal (*in casu* a head of cattle), that is, an animal owned by someone. The term used for the animal in this law (*shōr*) refers non-specifically to a head of cattle. It may refer to a cow, bull, or ox (i.e. a castrated bull). An ox was not acceptable for sacrifice, given its damaged or removed testicles (Lev. 22:24). The law of Leviticus shows that castration of bulls was known. The purpose was, of course, to provide for a more docile animal which could be used in ploughing or pulling carts. Relatively few bulls would have been kept, given that they were only needed for propagation or (an expensive form of) draught animal. Although a bull would be more likely to gore, oxen are also able to do so as are (horned) cows. In fact, cows were often used not only for milking and rearing young, but also for the jobs that oxen were used for, such as ploughing and drawing carts (this fact is presumed in the laws requiring cows which have never been yoked, cf. Num. 19:2; Deut. 21:3; 1 Sam. 6:7). On a smaller farm, keeping separate oxen for such jobs would have been too expensive. Two first century AD Greek epigrams illustrate what must have been the not uncommon practice of using a cow – even during the period when it was still giving suck to its calves – to plough the fields:[88]

---

88. The texts are cited from the edition of Gow and Page. The Greek is as follows:

Καὶ τὸν ἀρουραῖον γυρητόμον αὔλακα τέμνει
μηροτυπεῖ κέντρῳ πειθομένη δάμαλις
καὶ μετ' ἀροτροπόνους ζεύγλας πάλι τῷ νεοθηλεῖ
πινομένη μόσχῳ δεύτερον ἄλγος ἔχει.
μὴ θλίψῃς αὐτὴν ὁ γεωμόρος· οὗτος ὁ βαιός
μόσχος, ἐὰν φείσῃ, σοὶ τρέφεται δάμαλης. (Philip, *AP* 9.274)

Ἠνίδε καὶ χέρσου τὸ γεωτόμον ὅπλον ἐρέσσει
καὶ τὸν ὑπουθατίαν μόσχον ἄγει δάμαλις,
βούταν μὲν τρομέουσα διάκτορα, τὸν δὲ μένουσα
νήπιον, ἀμφυτέρων εὔστοχα φειδομένα.

"Obedient to thigh-smiting goad the cow cleaves the curve-cut furrow of the ploughland; and again, after the plough-labour under the yoke, suffers a second pain suckling her new-born calf. Strike her not, you ploughman there; this little calf, if you are merciful, will grow up for you a young ox (lit. 'bull-calf')." (Philip, *AP* 9.274)

"See how the heifer both speeds the land's earth-cleaving tool and leads her suckling calf. The driver-herdsman she dreads, yet lingers for her little one, careful of both, shrewd-guessing. Hold back, earth-delver, as you plough to and fro, press not hard upon her who bears the double burden of double tasks." (Bianor, *AP* 10.101)

Accidental death by goring

If the head of cattle in question kills someone, but there is no question of the owner realising that the animal was dangerous, there is no punishment to the owner. This accords with the basic principle that damage incurred by accident requires no restitution or punishment. The animal itself, however, must be killed and the owner is forbidden to eat it. These stipulations ought not to be viewed as a punishment of the owner, but as punishment for the animal itself. This much is suggested by the stipulated manner of death by stoning, a judicial form of death penalty. The head of cattle is punished in an exemplaric way for destroying a person who was made in the image of God (cf. Gen. 9:5-6).[89] In other words, the point is not that cattle are considered to be culpable moral beings, but that the stoning of the animal for murder ought to be a warning to people of the consequences of taking a human life.

A different view is taken by Houtman, who suggests that the reason the owner is not to eat of it is because the blood of the animal has not been drained according to the law of Leviticus 17. He views stoning not as a disciplinary death penalty, but the normal way of killing an

---

ἴσχε', ἀροτροδίαυλε, πεδώρυχε, μηδὲ διώξῃς
τὰν διπλοῖς ἔργοις διπλὰ βαρυνομέναν. (Bianor, *AP* 10.101)
89. Later rabbinic tradition also forbade the owner to make use of the skin (see Houtman).

animal that is dangerous. Several comments may be made on this view. In the first place, Houtman neglects to consider why a dangerous animal might not better be killed with a spear or a bow and arrow, just as wild animals were killed. In respect of eating it there are two considerations. Firstly, after death by stoning the blood could still surely be drained. Wild deer and gazelles must have been killed first (e.g. by spear) and only then had their blood drained. In the second place, there is the question as to whether the blood ritual of Leviticus 17 was already in force at this time.

This law may be compared and contrasted to that for accidental manslaughter. In the case of accidental manslaughter the perpetrator must flee to a city of refuge until the death of the high priest. He is still, in however small a degree, held responsible for the spilling of blood. It is clear that this is not the case when his domestic animal happens to kill someone. The same principle is applied in Western legal systems.

Negligent death by goring

When, however, the owner of the head of cattle ought to have realised that his animal was dangerous (for example, because it had gored other animals) and he had not taken due precautions,[90] he is liable to the death penalty if the animal kills another free person (adult or child, male or female). The death penalty is in lieu of the fact that the normal principle of restitution in the case of damage due to negligence cannot be applied. For this reason the death penalty is not compulsory. (Murder carries a compulsory death penalty because in that case death is a punishment, not a means to provide restitution for the family of the deceased). The accuser (the family of the deceased) may decide to accept a ransom payment in lieu of death. The absolute maximum amount he could ask would be the total asset value of the owner[91] plus six years wages (the maximum loan, which could be paid through debt slavery, cf. Exod. 21:2). We must assume, however, that the owner had

---

90. The LXX (reading a slightly different text at v.29, see the textual notes) translates "and (if) he (the owner) did not *destroy* it".
91. His land would not be included in the asset value as this in fact belonged to God himself.

the right to refuse to pay the ransom, in which case he would receive the death penalty.

The death of a slave (male or married female[92]) by negligence does not require the death penalty, but the owner of the slave must be compensated with a payment of 30 silver shekels.[93] The prosecutor in the case of the death of a slave is not his immediate family, but his owner. In this instance the law prevents the owner from using a death penalty threat to claim excessive compensation. Compensation for a dead slave killed in this way cannot be compared to compensation for a free person. This provision could be seen as a form of protection for slaves. If the master had the right to sue for a higher compensation, he may have been tempted to put his slaves unnecessarily in danger for their lives. Restitution is made according to an average value for the slave. An idea of the value of various categories of slaves can be gained from Leviticus 27:1-7.

Male 20-60 yrs	50 silver shekels
Female 20-60 yrs	30 silver shekels
Male 5-20 yrs	20 silver shekels
Female 5-20 yrs	10 silver shekels
Male 1 mth – 5 yrs	5 silver shekels
Female 1 mth – 5 yrs	3 silver shekels

The table shows that the fine must be considered an average compensation.[94] Although the question of the value of a shekel at

---

92. The LXX uses the terminology for regular (not household) slaves, given that domestic slaves would not normally be in the vicinity of cattle. The Hebrew restricts the female slave to one who is married (and therefore owned by a male) and is probably made for the same reason. Unmarried female slaves were owned by the mistress of the house and would unlikely be working in the open fields.
93. The reader will immediately realise that Judas' recompense for the betrayal of Jesus equates his value with that of a dead slave (Matt. 26:15).
94. The *codex Hammurabi* (§§ 250-52) has a similar law involving exactly the same cases in the same order, namely, a head of cattle which accidentally kills someone, a head of cattle known to be dangerous which kills someone, and a head of cattle known to be dangerous which kills a slave. The consequences are,

the time of Moses is difficult, the code of Hammurabi (*ca.* 1772 BC) suggests that the average annual wage of a day labourer (i.e. a person at the bottom of the earning scale) was 10 silver shekels.[95] By the time of the New Testament, however, a denarius (= 1 shekel) was considered to be a normal daily wage for a day labourer (Matt. 20:2). The amount required, however, remained fixed in Jewish law, unaffected by inflation. This meant that by New Testament times, recompense for a dead slave was a comparatively paltry sum.

The stipulation in verse 31 that the owner of the head of cattle must be punished whether the animal has gored an adult or a child is probably to be considered a warning against a common near Eastern custom. It tended to happen that a man was often punished for something he did against another's children, by having the same thing done to his own children.[96] This law specifically forbids that practice by ruling that the owner of the animal (and thus not his own children) must be punished. See also Deuteronomy 24:16.

Other laws addressing negligence

The principle that failure to take due precaution to protect one's neighbour from danger arising from one's own property makes the owner culpable is also further illustrated in God's law. In Deuteronomy 22:8 we read:

> *When you build a new house, you shall make a parapet for your roof, that you may not bring bloodguilt on your house if anyone falls from it.*

In ancient Israel the flat roofs of houses were used as outdoor patios. This required protection from falling off. The punishment for the death of someone who fell off one's roof, if it had not been protected, would be the same as for an unprotected dangerous head of cattle. In the

---

however, different. The first case is similar except for the fact that the animal is left alive. In the second and third cases only a specified financial penalty is applied.
95. De Vaux, 76.
96. For examples of this basic principle see the *codex Hammurabi* §§ 116, 209-210, 230.

same way, local by-laws in Western society compel citizens to protect dangerous property (e.g. railings around swimming pools, muzzles for dangerous breeds of dogs, use of safety belts for passengers in cars).

Text

²⁸ Ἐὰν δὲ κερατίσῃ ταῦρος ἄνδρα ἢ γυναῖκα, καὶ ἀποθάνῃ, λίθοις λιθοβοληθήσεται ὁ ταῦρος, καὶ οὐ βρωθήσεται τὰ κρέα αὐτοῦ· ὁ δὲ κύριος τοῦ ταύρου ἀθῷος ἔσται. ²⁹ ἐὰν δὲ ὁ ταῦρος κερατιστὴς ᾖ πρὸ τῆς ἐχθὲς καὶ πρὸ τῆς τρίτης, καὶ διαμαρτύρωνται τῷ κυρίῳ αὐτοῦ, καὶ μὴ ἀφανίσῃ αὐτόν, ἀνέλῃ δὲ ἄνδρα ἢ γυναῖκα, ὁ ταῦρος λιθοβοληθήσεται, καὶ ὁ κύριος αὐτοῦ προσαποθανεῖται. ³⁰ ἐὰν δὲ λύτρα ἐπιβληθῇ αὐτῷ, δώσει λύτρα τῆς ψυχῆς αὐτοῦ ὅσα ἂν ἐπιβάλωσιν αὐτῷ. ³¹ ἐὰν δὲ υἱὸν κερατίσῃ ἢ θυγατέρα, κατὰ τὸ δικαίωμα τοῦτο ποιήσουσιν αὐτῷ. ³² ἐὰν δὲ παῖδα κερατίσῃ ὁ ταῦρος ἢ παιδίσκην, ἀργυρίου τριάκοντα δίδραχμα δώσει τῷ κυρίῳ αὐτῶν, καὶ ὁ ταῦρος λιθοβοληθήσεται.

וְכִי־יִגַּח שׁוֹר אֶת־אִישׁ אוֹ אֶת־אִשָּׁה וָמֵת סָקוֹל יִסָּקֵל הַשּׁוֹר וְלֹא יֵאָכֵל אֶת־בְּשָׂרוֹ וּבַעַל הַשּׁוֹר נָקִי: ²⁹ וְאִם שׁוֹר נַגָּח הוּא מִתְּמֹל שִׁלְשֹׁם וְהוּעַד בִּבְעָלָיו וְלֹא יִשְׁמְרֶנּוּ וְהֵמִית אִישׁ אוֹ אִשָּׁה הַשּׁוֹר יִסָּקֵל וְגַם־בְּעָלָיו יוּמָת: ³⁰ אִם־כֹּפֶר יוּשַׁת עָלָיו וְנָתַן פִּדְיֹן נַפְשׁוֹ כְּכֹל אֲשֶׁר־יוּשַׁת עָלָיו: ³¹ אוֹ־בֵן יִגָּח אוֹ־בַת יִגָּח כַּמִּשְׁפָּט הַזֶּה יֵעָשֶׂה לּוֹ: ³² אִם־עֶבֶד יִגַּח הַשּׁוֹר אוֹ אָמָה כֶּסֶף שְׁלֹשִׁים שְׁקָלִים יִתֵּן לַאדֹנָיו וְהַשּׁוֹר יִסָּקֵל:

נגח, *Qal* to gore	נַגָּח, prone to gore (only used in this pericope)
סקל, *Qal* to stone	פִּדְי(וֹ)ן, redemption price (פדה, *Qal* to buy out, ransom)
עוד, *Hiph.* to be witness against + בְּ, *Hoph.* to be warned	κερατίζω, to butt with horns, gore (Jewish-Greek)

21:28

שׁוֹר / ταῦρος

The term שׁוֹר is non-specific and may refer to a cow, bull, or ox (= castrated bull). The LXX has, however, rendered the Hebrew more specifically in terms of a bull, probably considering that this animal is the most likely candidate for goring. Greek for a head of cattle is ὁ βοῦς.

אֶת־אִישׁ אוֹ אֶת־אִשָּׁה

The definite object marker is sometimes used to mark an indefinite object for the sake of clarity, cf. Jouön/Muraoka §125h.

וְלֹא יֵאָכֵל אֶת־בְּשָׂרוֹ

Impersonal passives take an accusative of the affected object. Although grammatically בְּשָׂרוֹ is not a direct object, it is *felt* to be that way, given that the impersonal passive substitutes for a transitive active verb ('and one may not eat its flesh'), cf. Jouön/Muraoka §128b.

21:29

מִתְּמֹל שִׁלְשֹׁם / πρὸ τῆς ἐχθὲς καὶ πρὸ τῆς τρίτης (*sc.* ἡμέρας)

A fixed idiom 'from yesterday and the day before', meaning 'for some time previously'.

וְהוּעַד / διαμαρτύρωνται

The LXX translates the impersonal passive *Hophal* correctly as an active plural verb in Greek, cf. v.30b (יוּשַׁת / ἐπιβάλωσιν), v.31b (יֵעָשֶׂה / ποιήσουσιν).

בִּבְעָלָיו ... וְגַם־בְּעָלָיו

Plurals of majesty going with a singular verb, cf. v.32 (לַאדֹנָיו).

יִשְׁמְרֶנּוּ / ἀφανίσῃ

The LXX reads ('destroy') יַשְׁמִדֶנּוּ.

יוּמָת / (προσ)αποθανεῖται

The LXX reads יָמוּת.

21:30

אִם / ἐὰν δὲ

On the question of a copulative, see the note to 21:4.

יוּשַׁת

Given that the verb שׁית is only elsewhere found in the *Qal*, this should be interpreted as a *Qal* passive and not a *Hophal* form.

21:31

אוֹ־בֵן יִגָּח אוֹ־בַת יִגָּח / ἐὰν δὲ υἱὸν κερατίσῃ ἢ θυγατέρα

Sc. אוֹ אִם בֵּן יִגָּח, cf. Joüon/Muraoka §167q. On the question of word-order Joüon/Muraoka is contradictory. On the one hand at §155o Exod. 21:31 is quoted as an example of placing the object first for emphasis, but at §155oc Exod. 21:31 is quoted as an example of placing the object first in legal texts with *no* added emphasis! Note the pausal lengthening of the first instance of the verb (*pathach* to *qametz*), which is a little unexpected at this point. It provides the effect of a comma. On the question of the Greek copulative, see the note to 21:4. The LXX may not have read the doubled verb, but this cannot be certain.

21:32

אִם־עֶבֶד יִגַּח הַשּׁוֹר אוֹ אָמָה / ἐὰν δὲ παῖδα κερατίσῃ ὁ ταῦρος ἢ παιδίσκην

For the word-order see the comment at v.31. On the question of an initial copulative, see the note to 21:4. The LXX uses the terminology for regular slaves, given that domestic slaves would not normally be in the vicinity of cattle. The restriction of a female slave to one who is married (and therefore owned by a male) is probably made for the same reason. Unmarried female slaves were owned by the mistress of the house and would unlikely be working in the open fields.

שְׁקָלִים / δίδραχμα

On the value of the temple shekel see Anderson[11].

21:33-34

Death of another's animal in one's uncovered pit

Translation

³³ And when someone opens a pit or when someone digs a pit and he does not cover it and a head of cattle or a donkey falls in it,

³⁴ then the owner of the pit will make reparation, in return he will give money to its owner and the dead animal will be his.

Commentary

The principle here is once again that damage caused to another's property due to one's own negligence ought to be reimbursed. The damaged goods become the property of the perpetrator because in the sense of this law he purchases the dead animal for the price it was worth when it was living. A similar situation arises when one borrows property from another and it becomes damaged while the owner is absent (22:14).

It is interesting to note that the law does not specify who in fact left the pit open, but speaks of 'someone' (v.33). In every case it is the responsibility of the 'owner' of the pit to make restitution. This implies that the owner is responsible for the activities of his workers, wife or children.

The dead beast, both here and in the next law, becomes the property of the owner of the pit. The law of Deuteronomy 14:21, however, restricts its use.

> *You shall not eat anything that has died naturally. You may give it to the sojourner who is within your towns, that he may eat it,*

or you may sell it to a foreigner. For you are a people holy to the LORD your God.

The skin could be used for leather, the fat could be used for various purposes, however the animal could not be eaten. The meat could be sold to a foreigner or given to a resident alien unconcerned with worshipping YHWH.

Text

³³ Ἐὰν δέ τις ἀνοίξῃ λάκκον ἢ λατομήσῃ λάκκον καὶ μὴ καλύψῃ αὐτόν, καὶ ἐμπέσῃ ἐκεῖ μόσχος ἢ ὄνος, ³⁴ ὁ κύριος τοῦ λάκκου ἀποτείσει· ἀργύριον δώσει τῷ κυρίῳ αὐτῶν, τὸ δὲ τετελευτηκὸς αὐτῷ ἔσται	וְכִי־יִפְתַּח אִישׁ בּוֹר אוֹ כִּי־יִכְרֶה אִישׁ בֹּר וְלֹא יְכַסֶּנּוּ וְנָפַל־שָׁמָּה שּׁוֹר אוֹ חֲמוֹר: ³⁴ בַּעַל הַבּוֹר יְשַׁלֵּם כֶּסֶף יָשִׁיב לִבְעָלָיו וְהַמֵּת יִהְיֶה־לּוֹ:

כרה, *Qal* to hollow out, dig	λάκκος, ὁ, pit, tank, cistern, vat (for storing water, wine, etc.)

21:33

יִכְרֶה / λατομήσῃ

The LXX is more specific, suggesting that any pit would certainly be hewn out of rock.

שׁוֹר אוֹ חֲמוֹר / μόσχος ἢ ὄνος

The LXX renders the 'head of cattle' as a 'calf' (which in Hebrew would be a עֵגֶל), perhaps thinking that a full size head of cattle would not likely fall into a pit.

Note the *daghesh forte conjunctivum* in שׁוֹר helping the enunciation of the שׁ after a ה.

21:34

לִבְעָלָיו / τῷ κυρίῳ αὐτῶν

Again the Hebrew uses a plural of majesty. The LXX once again renders the pronominal suffix plural to match the two animals.

21:35-36

One's head of cattle kills another man's head of cattle

Translation

³⁵ And when someone's head of cattle strikes the head of cattle of his neighbour and it dies, then they will sell the live animal and divide its proceeds and the dead animal too they will divide.

³⁶ And if it was known that a head of cattle was prone to gore previously[97] and its owner did not guard it[98], then he shall surely recompense a head of cattle for a head of cattle and the dead animal will belong to him.

Commentary

The first part of this law provides an exception to the legal principle that accidental damage does not require restitution. In this case the result of the damage is divided between the two parties. This exception is confined to cattle causing the death of other cattle. Cattle were expensive animals essential to the livelihood of their owners. While lesser damage would not have to be compensated, the accidental loss of a head of cattle could have more serious consequences. We should bear in mind that the sharing of the expense of the damage helps to prevent a case of accidental damage turning a neighbour over to financial ruin in an economy without accident insurance.

The second part of this law is yet another application of the principle involved in the previous laws. The owner of property (*in casu* a head

---
97. *Lit.* "from yesterday and the day before" – an idiom for 'previously'.
98. Alternately, following the LXX, "and its owner had been warned and he did not destroy it".

of cattle) which he knows to be dangerous is responsible for reparation when another's property is damaged by it.[99]

Early rabbinic tradition interpreted the principles taught in this law in a different way. They saw the law as teaching a distinction between injury caused by things which are ranked as 'harmless' and things which are an 'attested danger'. The ox in this law functions only as an example. This is in effect made explicit in the more expansive text of the Samaritan Pentateuch, which refers in addition to any animal. From this the principle is derived that damage caused by something ranked as 'harmless' should be divided between the owner of that which caused the damage and the owner of the damaged goods. Conversely, damage caused by something ranked as an 'attested danger' should be fully compensated by the owner of whatever caused the damage.[100] In addition, the tradition ruled that the word 'neighbour' in this law only applies to an Israelite. The ox of a Gentile which is killed by the ox of an Israelite does not have to be recompensed, neither does an ox belonging to the temple have to be recompensed. Conversely, however, a Gentile whose ox kills the ox of an Israelite must make full reparation.[101]

---

99. If he knew it to be dangerous, then according to the MT he should have kept it in safe custody (שמר), but according to the LXX he should have destroyed it (שמד). See the textual notes.
100. See Mishnah, *Baba Kamma*.
101. Mishnah, *Baba Kamma* 4.3.

Text

³⁵ Ἐὰν δὲ κερατίσῃ τινὸς ταῦρος τὸν ταῦρον τοῦ πλησίον, καὶ τελευτήσῃ, ἀποδώσονται τὸν ταῦρον τὸν ζῶντα καὶ διελοῦνται τὸ ἀργύριον αὐτοῦ, καὶ τὸν ταῦρον τὸν τεθνηκότα διελοῦνται. ³⁶ ἐὰν δὲ γνωρίζηται ὁ ταῦρος ὅτι κερατιστής ἐστιν πρὸ τῆς ἐχθὲς καὶ πρὸ τῆς τρίτης ἡμέρας, καὶ διαμεμαρτυρημένοι ὦσιν τῷ κυρίῳ αὐτοῦ, καὶ μὴ ἀφανίσῃ αὐτόν, ἀποτείσει ταῦρον ἀντὶ ταύρου, ὁ δὲ τετελευτηκὼς αὐτῷ ἔσται.	וְכִי־יִגֹּף שׁוֹר־אִישׁ אֶת־שׁוֹר רֵעֵהוּ וָמֵת וּמָכְרוּ אֶת־הַשּׁוֹר הַחַי וְחָצוּ אֶת־כַּסְפּוֹ וְגַם אֶת־הַמֵּת יֶחֱצוּן: ³⁶ אוֹ נוֹדַע כִּי שׁוֹר נַגָּח הוּא מִתְּמוֹל שִׁלְשֹׁם וְלֹא יִשְׁמְרֶנּוּ בְּעָלָיו שַׁלֵּם יְשַׁלֵּם שׁוֹר תַּחַת הַשּׁוֹר וְהַמֵּת יִהְיֶה־לּוֹ:

21:35

וְכִי־יִגֹּף שׁוֹר־אִישׁ / Ἐὰν δὲ κερατίσῃ τινὸς ταῦρος

The verb נגף had been used above in v.22 of men fighting and accidentally *striking* a pregnant woman. It is curious that the Hebrew verb for goring used above is not used here again. However, it should be noted that the cognate Akkadian word *nakāpu* is also used for goring cattle in legal texts.[102] Is the LXX an interpretation or did it read נגח? On the LXX use of ταῦρος, see the textual notes to 21:28.

אֶת־שׁוֹר רֵעֵהוּ / τὸν ταῦρον τοῦ πλησίον

The lack of the personal pronoun in the LXX may be purely stylistic, given that it is implied by the definite article in the Greek. The Hebrew אֶת־ (represented by the definite article in Greek) requires the personal pronoun in lieu of the definite article.

21:36

אוֹ / ἐὰν δὲ

The LXX seems not to have read a paragogic *nun* at the end of v.35, but to have taken this as a *waw* and read וְאִם. This reading makes

---

102. Cf. *Assyrian Dictionary* (ed. Roth).

much more sense given that a different situation is discussed here. See, however, the textual note to 21:4.

וְלֹא יִשְׁמְרֶנּוּ בְּעָלָיו שַׁלֵּם יְשַׁלֵּם / καὶ διαμεμαρτυρημένοι ὦσιν τῷ κυρίῳ αὐτοῦ, καὶ μὴ ἀφανίσῃ αὐτόν, ἀποτείσει

The LXX has read: וְהוּעַד בִּבְעָלָיו וְלֹא יִשְׁמְדֶנּוּ יְשַׁלֵּם, cf. v.29 (with notes). The slight difference in the translation of the similar passage indicates that that this not a Greek harmonisation (*contra* Wevers), but a translation of a different Hebrew *Vorlage*. Both here and in v.29 the reading of the LXX would require the owner of a goring ox to kill it, not just to ensure it is fenced in.

Note that the periphrastic construction in the indicative mood usually only occurs for the perfect or pluperfect middle/pass. indicative 3rd person plural of stems ending in a consonant. In those cases the perfect uses the midd./pass. participle + present tense εἰσί while the pluperfect uses the past tense ἦσαν. However, for the subjunctive mood the periphrastic construction is almost always used.

שׁוֹר תַּחַת הַשּׁוֹר / ταῦρον ἀντὶ ταύρου

The LXX is probably correct here and the definite article in the Hebrew, which is not idiomatic in this context, is likely to be a scribal error.

22:1-4 (Hebr. 21:37 – 22:3)

Theft of animals

Translation

²²:¹ When someone steals an animal from the herd or the flock and he slaughters it or sells it, for the head of cattle he will make fivefold reparation in cattle and for the animal from the flock he will make fourfold reparation from the flock.

² (If the thief is discovered during the burglary and he is struck and dies, there is no blood-guilt for him.

³ If the sun rises upon him there is blood-guilt for him.) He will surely make reparation. If he is penniless, then he is to be sold for the stolen animal.

⁴ If the stolen animal is truly found in his possession[103] alive, whether from the herd or even unto a donkey or an animal from the flock, he shall make double reparation.

Commentary

Theft of animals from the herd or flock: A special case

Several principles are at play in this law. The theft of cattle or sheep (or goats[104]) involves a modification of the general penalty for theft as outlined in 22:7 and 9, namely that the thief pay double the value of what he stole. When applied to cattle or sheep/goats this double repayment only applies if the original animal is recovered undamaged. If it has been otherwise disposed of the thief must reimburse cattle

---

103. Lit. 'in his hand'.
104. The Hebrew term (שֶׂה) is generic for an animal from the flock, whether sheep or goat.

fivefold and sheep/goats fourfold, cf. 2 Samuel 12:1-6. If he is unable to pay, he may be sold into slavery until the debt is satisfied, that is, the sale price will be commensurate with his debt and thus determine the length of his service in slavery (see on Exod. 21,2 for the maximum service).[105]

Of interest is the fact that Josephus mistakes this law as if fourfold restitution was the punishment for all theft (*Ant.* 16.3). Zaccheus may have been under the same general misconception when he promised: "if I have defrauded anyone of anything, I restore it fourfold" (Luke 19:8). Both Zaccheus and Josephus, however, were probably influenced by Roman law which demanded fourfold restitution for extortion.[106] This misinterpretation of God's law was, however, not necessarily generally accepted at that time. Philo, around the beginning of the first century, interprets the law correctly as does the third century AD Mishnah.[107]

The main question here is why cattle and sheep/goats are reimbursed in such large amounts. It might be claimed that these animals, in distinction to other domestic beasts, are reckoned by the law of Moses to be clean domestic animals, that is, suitable for sacrifice. Not all such animals, however, would have been suitable. Apart from the requirement that an animal be unblemished, some cattle were deliberately castrated to function as draught oxen. Donkeys (mentioned only in v.4), however, seem to be excluded from four or fivefold restitution. The point of mentioning donkeys in verse 4 would seem to be underscoring that when cattle or sheep/goats are found intact the normal reparation is made, namely twofold. When

---

105. The *codex Hammurabi* (§8) makes theft much more serious, requiring such large reparations that most thieves will have faced the death penalty. A thief who is caught in the act or who has dug a hole through a wall also faces the death penalty (§§21-22). No distinction is made between livestock or other kinds of property. The law at §8 reads: "If a man has stolen an ox, or a sheep, or a donkey, or a pig, or a boat [*sic.* an error for 'goat'] he shall pay thirty times its value if it belongs to a god or a temple [Richardson notes that 'palace' is another possibility] and repay ten times its value if it belongs to a workman. If that thief does not have enough to pay he shall be killed.". (transl. Richardson).
106. See Horsley, entry 23, p.72f.
107. Philo, *Spec.Leg.* 4.2; Mishnah, *Baba Kamma* 7:1.

cattle or sheep/goats specifically (implying the exclusion of other domestic animals) are not recovered, *their* reparation is much higher. One might argue that the increased reparation for animals from the herd or flock has to do with the fact that these animals represent the staple products of one's livelihood in an agricultural community. A final question is why the penalty is less (twofold reparation) if the animals are found alive in the thief's possession. In this scenario, the owner naturally receives his very own animal(s) back. Houtman adds the consideration that in this case it is unclear if the person in whose possession the animals are found was actually the thief, or, perhaps instead was someone who found (or even obtained?) the animals and decided to keep them for himself. These considerations do not seem to me to amount to much, particularly when this law is put next to that on kidnapping (Exod. 21:16). A thief of persons (i.e. a kidnapper) receives the maximum penalty whether or not the stolen goods were recovered intact. This surely has to do with the fact that kidnapping involves persons made in the image of God.

Catching a thief

The second principle concerns how far the owner can go when trying to prevent or catch a thief of cattle or sheep/goats. The law makes it plain that the owner should not set out to kill the thief. Daylight should provide him with enough means to prevent this. During the night the owner is given the benefit of the doubt. Daylight ('if the sun has risen') is contrasted with 'digging through' (often translated simply as 'breaking-in'). The standard way of breaking and entering in ancient times was digging through a wall. This was an activity associated with a break-in at night.[108] If the thief he is trying to catch dies from blows made during the darkness of night, there is no bloodguilt. Whether or not this principle only applies to a thief of cattle or sheep/goats, or to all cases of theft is not made clear. Jeremiah, however, implies that it was applied to all cases of theft. He alludes to this law and

---

108. Here in Western Australia it is also permitted to detain a thief using only as much force as is necessary. Up until some 15 years ago it was legal to shoot a thief in the process of attempting to detain him (he did not need to be an actual threat to warrant shooting).

presupposes that such thieves would be poor people. The wealthy women in Jerusalem are accused of killing the poor even when they were *not* breaking in at night:

> *Also on your skirts is found the lifeblood of the guiltless poor; you did not find them breaking in.* (Jer. 2:34)

Text

³⁷ Ἐὰν δέ τις κλέψῃ μόσχον ἢ πρόβατον, καὶ σφάξῃ αὐτὸ ἢ ἀποδῶται, πέντε μόσχους ἀποτείσει ἀντὶ τοῦ μόσχου καὶ τέσσαρα πρόβατα ἀντὶ τοῦ προβάτου. 22 ἐὰν δὲ ἐν τῷ διορύγματι εὑρεθῇ ὁ κλέπτης, καὶ πληγεὶς ἀποθάνῃ, οὐκ ἔστιν αὐτῷ φόνος· ² ἐὰν δὲ ἀνατείλῃ ὁ ἥλιος ἐπ' αὐτῷ, ἔνοχός ἐστιν, ἀνταποθανεῖται. ἐὰν δὲ μὴ ὑπάρχῃ αὐτῷ, πραθήτω ἀντὶ τοῦ κλέμματος. ³ ἐὰν δὲ καταλημφθῇ, καὶ εὑρεθῇ ἐν τῇ χειρὶ αὐτοῦ τὸ κλέμμα ἀπό τε ὄνου ἕως προβάτου ζῶντα, διπλᾶ αὐτὰ ἀποτείσει.	כִּי יִגְנֹב־אִישׁ שׁוֹר אוֹ־שֶׂה וּטְבָחוֹ אוֹ מְכָרוֹ חֲמִשָּׁה בָקָר יְשַׁלֵּם תַּחַת הַשּׁוֹר וְאַרְבַּע־צֹאן תַּחַת הַשֶּׂה: 22 ¹ אִם־בַּמַּחְתֶּרֶת יִמָּצֵא הַגַּנָּב וְהֻכָּה וָמֵת אֵין לוֹ דָּמִים: ² אִם־זָרְחָה הַשֶּׁמֶשׁ עָלָיו דָּמִים לוֹ שַׁלֵּם יְשַׁלֵּם אִם־אֵין לוֹ וְנִמְכַּר בִּגְנֵבָתוֹ: ³ אִם־הִמָּצֵא תִמָּצֵא בְיָדוֹ הַגְּנֵבָה מִשּׁוֹר עַד־חֲמוֹר עַד־שֶׂה חַיִּים שְׁנַיִם יְשַׁלֵּם:

טבח, to slaughter	זרח, to rise
מַחְתֶּרֶת, break-in, burglary (used 2x, cf. חתר, to dig)	גְּנֵבָה, stolen object (only used in this passage)

21:37

כִּי יִגְנֹב־אִישׁ / Ἐὰν δέ τις κλέψῃ

The LXX may have read וְכִי (also the reading of Sam. Pent.), but given that we have the introduction of a new law here, this seems an unlikely reading. See the textual note to 21:4.

22:1

אִם / ἐὰν δὲ

On the question of a copulative here and twice in 22:2, see the note to 21:4.

22:2

דָּמִים לוֹ שַׁלֵּם יְשַׁלֵּם / ἔνοχός ἐστιν, ἀνταποθανεῖται.

The LXX takes the Hebrew verbal phrase with the preceding implying the use of the principle of *talio* against the killer of the thief (manslaughter with intent to harm being equivalent to murder). In context, however, the phrase makes more sense with what follows, implying the thief as the subject. It is followed by two conditional clauses. This was also the interpretation of the *Naqdanim* (i.e., the 7th century AD Tiberian Jews, who devised the system of pointing used here) who placed an *athnach* under the preceding לוֹ.

וְנִמְכַּר / πραθήτω

The copulative may have been omitted in translation for the sense.

22:2-3

אִם בִּגְנֵבָתוֹ: אִם / ἀντὶ τοῦ κλέμματος. ἐὰν **δὲ**

The LXX may well be correct in taking the *waw* as a conjunction belonging with the next verse. Note that גְּנֵבָה is one of several feminine nouns which retain the long *e* under inflection, and thus בִּגְנֵבָתוֹ, not as might have been expected: בִּגְנֵבָתוֹ.

22:3

אִם־הִמָּצֵא תִמָּצֵא / ἐὰν δὲ καταλημφθῇ, καὶ εὑρεθῇ

The LXX may just have read: וְאִם־נִמְצָא וְתִמָּצֵא. On the question of the initial copulative, see, however, the textual note to 21:4.

מִשּׁוֹר עַד־חֲמוֹר עַד־שֶׂה / ἀπό τε ὄνου ἕως προβάτου

By omitting the animal from the herd, the LXX seems to imply that an exception is made for a larger animal and even if retrieved alive, it should be repaid fivefold. However the τε seems out of place, which may suggest corruption in the Greek text.

22:5 (Hebr. 22:4)

Accidental grazing of another's field

Translation

⁵ When someone causes (his livestock) to graze off a field or vineyard and allows his livestock to go free and they graze in another's field, he will surely make reparation from his own field according to its produce, and if he causes (his livestock) to graze off the whole field, he shall make reparation with the best of his own field and the best of his own vineyard.

Commentary

This law and the following law, like those of 22:7-13 following, belong together although only one of them actually concerns animals. These two laws concern damage to a farmer's field, first through livestock and second through fire.

The text of this first law in the Samaritan Pentateuch, Septuagint and Qumran show that the Massoretic text has skipped a line. The NKJV and ESV wrongly follow the Masoretic text in their translations.

The principle here is one of restitution and not of penalisation. It would seem therefore that *intent to misuse* another man's field cannot be proven (otherwise it would be tantamount to theft and require double restitution). Houtman suggests a scenario whereby a farmer whose crop has been harvested allows his animals to freely graze the land, however they wander over to a neighbour's field whose crop has not yet been harvested. The question, which the law addresses concerns the quality of the crop to be restored by the owner of the animal(s) which got loose. If the animal(s) only grazed part of a field, he is to restore the crop with normal (average) quality goods. If his animal ruined an entire field (increasing his culpability for not realising the problem sooner), he is to restore the damaged crop with the best of his own crop.

Hopkins has argued that the intent of allowing animals to graze a field would be to deliberately distribute manure upon a field which was allowed to lie fallow for a year.[109] He has shown that it would more than likely be the case that a farmer in antiquity would allow half of his land to lie fallow and to harvest crops on the other half, alternating year by year (see further the commentary to 23:10-11). The scenario envisaged in this case law is where the animals grazing a fallow field manage to escape, attracted by the food offered from the crops of a neighbour's field.

In both this case and the next there is a degree of negligence which caused the accidental damage. This is the reason why complete restitution is required, which was not the case with the pure accident of Exodus 21:35 where the damage was shared between the two parties.

Text

⁴ Ἐὰν δὲ καταβοσκήσῃ τις ἀγρὸν ἢ ἀμπελῶνα, καὶ ἀφῇ τὸ κτῆνος αὐτοῦ καταβοσκῆσαι ἀγρὸν ἕτερον, ἀποτείσει ἐκ τοῦ ἀγροῦ αὐτοῦ κατὰ τὸ γένημα αὐτοῦ. ἐὰν δὲ πάντα τὸν ἀγρὸν καταβοσκήσῃ, τὰ βέλτιστα τοῦ ἀγροῦ αὐτοῦ ἢ τὰ βέλτιστα τοῦ ἀμπελῶνος αὐτοῦ ἀποτείσει.	כִּי יַבְעֶר־אִישׁ שָׂדֶה אוֹ־כֶרֶם וְשִׁלַּח אֶת־בְּעִירֹה וּבִעֵר בִּשְׂדֵה אַחֵר [שַׁלֵּם יְשַׁלֵּם מִשָּׂדֵהוּ כִּתְבוּאָתוֹ וְאִם כָּל־הַשָּׂדֶה יַבְעֶר] מֵיטַב שָׂדֵהוּ וּמֵיטַב כַּרְמוֹ יְשַׁלֵּם:

109. Hopkins, 206-207.

בער I. *Qal* to burn; *Hiph.* to cause to burn II. (probably etymologically unrelated homonym) *Piel* to graze; *Hiph.* to cause to be grazed (only used 2x)	בְּעִיר, livestock שׁלח, *Qal* to send; *Piel* to let go free מֵיטָב, the best (part) καταβόσκω, feed flocks upon

22:4

כִּי / Ἐὰν δὲ

> On the question of a copulative, see the textual note to 21:37. Sam. Pent. reads וכי.

יַבְעֶר

> Given that the *Hiphil* is only used twice, some scholars suggest that it may be better to read the *Piel* here: יְבַעֵר. Jenni[2] (239), however, argues that we have a regular causative *Hiphil* here, with the object as self-explanatory (cattle) assumed: 'When a man causes (his cattle) to graze off a field …'

בְּעִירֹה / τὸ κτῆνος αὐτοῦ

> The *Naqdanim* (together with the LXX and Sam. Pent.) have pointed for בְּעִירוֹ, i.e. "another field" instead of "another's field". The consonants represent a 3rd pers. fem. suffix or an archaic spelling of the 3rd pers. masc. suffix.

בִּשְׂדֵה אַחֵר / ἀγρὸν ἕτερον

> The LXX has read: בְּשָׂדֶה אַחֵר.

[שַׁלֵּם יְשַׁלֵּם מִשָּׂדֵהוּ כִּתְבוּאָתוֹ וְאִם כָּל־הַשָּׂדֶה יַבְעֶר] / ἀποτείσει ἐκ τοῦ ἀγροῦ αὐτοῦ κατὰ τὸ γένημα αὐτοῦ. ἐὰν δὲ πάντα τὸν ἀγρὸν καταβοσκήσῃ

> The added consonantal text is from the Sam.Pent. with one small change. The pointing is my own. The Sam. Pent. reads יבעה for יבער (against the LXX, which is surely correct). The Qumran evidence is fragmentary, but shows clearly that the additional text was present. See Sanderson, 76-77. For the textual problem, see the main commentary.

22:6 (Hebr. 22:5)

Damage caused by out of control fire

Translation

⁶ When fire breaks out and finds thorny bushes and a heap of sheaves or the standing grain or the field is consumed, the person who caused the burning of that which is burned shall surely make reparation.

Commentary

The point here is that damage caused by the *accidental* spread of fire ought to be fully recompensed. Obviously crops set on fire deliberately would be a separate matter (cf. Judg. 15:5; 2 Sam. 14:30). Nevertheless, the inability to control a fire which one has started implies some degree of negligence. Fire was used both to clear bush for grazing domestic animals[110] and also to burn stubble after a grain harvest had been winnowed as the image of John the baptist illustrates:

> ¹⁵ As the people were in expectation, and all were questioning in their hearts concerning John, whether he might be the Christ, ¹⁶ John answered them all, saying, "I baptize you with water, but he who is mightier than I is coming, the strap of whose sandals I am not worthy to untie. He will baptize you with the Holy Spirit and fire. ¹⁷ His winnowing fork is in his hand, to clear his threshing floor and to gather the wheat into his barn, but the chaff he will burn with unquenchable fire." (Luke 3:15-17)

---

110. Hopkins, 116-17.

Text

| ⁵ Ἐὰν δὲ ἐξελθὸν πῦρ εὕρῃ ἀκάνθας, καὶ προσεμπρήσῃ ἅλωνα ἢ στάχυς ἢ πεδίον, ἀποτείσει ὁ τὸ πῦρ ἐκκαύσας. | כִּי־תֵצֵא אֵשׁ וּמָצְאָה קֹצִים וְנֶאֱכַל גָּדִישׁ אוֹ הַקָּמָה אוֹ הַשָּׂדֶה שַׁלֵּם יְשַׁלֵּם הַמַּבְעִר אֶת־הַבְּעֵרָה׃ |

| קוֹץ, thorny bushes | קָמָה, grain still on the stalk |
| גָּדִישׁ, heap of sheaves | בְּעֵרָה, that which is burned |

22:5

כִּי / Ἐὰν δὲ

On the question of a copulative, see the textual note to 21:4.

שַׁלֵּם יְשַׁלֵּם הַמַּבְעִר אֶת־הַבְּעֵרָה / ἀποτείσει ὁ τὸ πῦρ ἐκκαύσας

The last clause of the verse ought to be translated: "he who caused the burning of that which is burned shall surely make reparation". The object of the *Hiphil* בער ('to cause to be burning') regularly denotes that which is burned. The noun בְּעֵרָה is a *hapax legomenon* in the Old Testament, but is parallel to גְּנֵבָה ('that which is stolen') and אֲבֵדָה ('that which is lost') in the same chapter. See Jenni[2], 81. The LXX may not have read the infinitive absolute.

22:7-9 (Hebr. 22:6-8)

Theft of inanimate property in one's keeping

Translation

⁷ When someone gives his neighbour money or vessels for safekeeping and there is a theft from his house, if the thief is found he shall make double reparation.

⁸ If the thief is not found then the master of the house shall be brought to the gods (to determine) whether he has not stretched forth his hand against the goods of his neighbour.

⁹ Concerning every property offence, concerning an animal from the herd, concerning a donkey, concerning an animal from the flock, concerning a cloak, concerning every lost thing of which someone says "(No, but) this is it!", the matter of the two of them will go as far as the gods. He whom the gods show to be guilty shall make twofold reparation to his neighbour.

Commentary

Just as the previous two laws, so also this law and the following law need to be taken together. Both deal with property held in safekeeping by someone. Although the theme of this section of the laws seems to be that of laws relating to animals, the first case law dealing with theft of inanimate property in one's keeping serves to highlight the differences between inanimate property and animals held in safekeeping.

The property concerned in this case law has not been borrowed. It was given for safekeeping. One can easily envisage a family needing to take a trip to the temple, for example, and leaving certain goods or animals in safekeeping with a neighbour. If upon return that which was deposited for safekeeping has genuinely been stolen, there is no reason for the person who kept it to recompense the owner. He was only doing him a favour in the first place.[111] A thief, if caught, must pay the normal fine of double the value of what was stolen. This is a simple application of the *lex talionis*, namely, what he stole from another is taken away from him.[112] It is not immediately clear from the text whether the penalty is paid to the original owner or the safekeeper from whose house it was taken. It is surely the latter for he is the one who has to take the trouble to find the thief and endures the stress related to the theft. This supposition is confirmed by the following law where we read that if a theft has definitely been established (that is, the thief is found), then the safekeeper should pay restitution to the owner. This implies that the safekeeper himself is able to claim the restitution and penalty from the thief.

If the thief is not found, the judges may investigate the possibility that the safekeeper has secretly stolen the goods. Verse 9 makes it clear that such an investigation only proceeds when the owner of the goods accuses the safekeeper of having stolen his property.

Several matters are of interest here. First, there is the term *^{e}lōhîm* (rendered 'gods') used in both verse 8 and verse 9. This word, coupled with a plural verb (as is the case in v.9), must be translated 'gods'. The context, however, prevents a reference to pagan gods and therefore refers here to the judges who are given a title of majesty.[113] For this use of the word *^{e}lōhîm* see the discussion in the introduction under the subheading 'Legal courts'.

---

111. The *codex Hammurabi*, in contrast, requires the safekeeper to recompense the stolen goods (§ 125). The consequent risk involved in storing another's goods would no doubt inhibit people from doing this as a mere favour.
112. The *codex Hammurabi*, in contrast, allows one who catches a thief in the act to kill him there and then (§§ 21-22).
113. Chirichigno's suggestion (238-40) that the reference here is to an oath in the sanctuary follows the understanding of the LXX (see below), but makes little sense. If an oath has been sworn the matter is given to God and no human penalty need ever be applied (contra v.9b).

A different interpretation is presupposed by the Septuagint translation, which reads in verses 7 and 8:

> *⁷ But if the thief is not found, the master of the house will come before God and swear that he has not acted wickedly against the whole of the entrusted property of his neighbour. ⁸ According to every specified wrong concerning a calf or a beast of burden or a sheep or a cloak or every lost thing which is prosecuted, whatever it should be, the judgment of both will come before God and the one who is taken by God will pay double to his neighbour.* (my translation)

On this reading, which rather strains the Hebrew at points (see the textual notes), both the safekeeper and he who accuses him of stealing his property must come before God. The accused safekeeper must swear an oath of purgation. Further, the fact that one of them is "taken by God" implies the use of Urim and Thumim to determine the guilty party.

In the second place, if the judges determine that the safekeeper *had* stolen the property, he is treated as a thief and must recompense double. However, the law makes it clear that even in the case of an ox or sheep he only needs to pay double. The supposition is that the animal is found alive and well (see 22:1-4).

Text

⁶ Ἐὰν δέ τις δῷ τῷ πλησίον ἀργύριον ἢ σκεύη φυλάξαι, καὶ κλαπῇ ἐκ τῆς οἰκίας τοῦ ἀνθρώπου, ἐὰν εὑρεθῇ ὁ κλέψας, ἀποτείσει διπλοῦν· ⁷ ἐὰν δὲ μὴ εὑρεθῇ ὁ κλέψας, προσελεύσεται ὁ κύριος τῆς οἰκίας ἐνώπιον τοῦ θεοῦ, καὶ ὀμεῖται, ἦ μὴν μὴ αὐτὸς πεπονη-ρεῦσθαι ἐφ' ὅλης τῆς παρακαταθήκης τοῦ πλησίον. ⁸ κατὰ πᾶν ῥητὸν ἀδίκημα περί τε μόσχου καὶ ὑποζυγίου καὶ προβάτου καὶ ἱματίου καὶ πάσης ἀπωλείας τῆς ἐγκαλουμένης, ὅ τι οὖν ἂν ᾖ, ἐνώπιον τοῦ θεοῦ ἐλεύσεται ἡ κρίσις ἀμφοτέρων, καὶ ὁ ἁλοὺς διὰ τοῦ θεοῦ ἀποτείσει διπλοῦν τῷ πλησίον.	כִּי־יִתֵּן אִישׁ אֶל־רֵעֵהוּ כֶּסֶף אוֹ־כֵלִים לִשְׁמֹר וְגֻנַּב מִבֵּית הָאִישׁ אִם־יִמָּצֵא הַגַּנָּב יְשַׁלֵּם שְׁנָיִם: ⁷ אִם־לֹא יִמָּצֵא הַגַּנָּב וְנִקְרַב בַּעַל־הַבַּיִת אֶל־הָאֱלֹהִים אִם־לֹא שָׁלַח יָדוֹ בִּמְלֶאכֶת רֵעֵהוּ: ⁸ עַל־כָּל־דְּבַר־פֶּשַׁע עַל־שׁוֹר עַל־חֲמוֹר עַל־שֶׂה עַל־שַׂלְמָה עַל־כָּל־אֲבֵדָה אֲשֶׁר יֹאמַר כִּי־הוּא זֶה עַד הָאֱלֹהִים יָבֹא דְּבַר־שְׁנֵיהֶם אֲשֶׁר יַרְשִׁיעֻן אֱלֹהִים יְשַׁלֵּם שְׁנַיִם לְרֵעֵהוּ:
גנב, *Qal* to steal; *Piel* to appropriate by theft (resultative)	παρακαταθήκη, ἡ, deposit of money or property entrusted to one's care
מְלָאכָה, work; objects, wares	ῥητός, ή, όν, (ἐρῶ) stated, specified
פֶּשַׁע, offence concerning property; crime	ἀπώλεια, ἡ, destruction; loss
אֲבֵדָה, lost property (אבד, to become lost; perish)	

22:6

כִּי־יִתֵּן אִישׁ / Ἐὰν δέ τις δῷ

On the question of a copulative, see the textual note to 21:37. Sam. Pent. reads וכי.

22:7

אִם־לֹא / ἐὰν δὲ μὴ

See the textual note to 21:4. Sam. Pent. reads ואם.

וְנִקְרַב / προσελεύσεται

The *Qal* means 'to draw near', the *Hiphil* 'to bring near'. The *Niphal* is only used twice in the OT. Although it is generally presumed that the *Niphal* is used as the active/passive middle voice of the *Qal*, we ought not to forget that it frequently functions as the active/passive middle voice of the *Hiphil*. Surely the latter is the case here. The safekeeper is to brought near to the 'gods'. He is unlikely to come unless summoned. The LXX appears to have read: יִקְרַב.

אִם־לֹא שָׁלַח יָדוֹ / καὶ ὀμεῖται, ἦ μὴν μὴ κτλ.

The LXX appears to have read: וְנִשְׁבַּע אִם־לֹא. The MT text is not an oath formula, but an indirect question. The phrase presupposes a verbal form such as לָדַעַת (from ידע), cf. Jouön/Muraoka §161f. Note the omission of אֶת before יָדוֹ, which is not uncommon when the direct object is a body-part, cf. Jouön/Muraoka §125ia.

בִּמְלָאכֶת / ἐφ' ὅλης τῆς παρακαταθήκης

The LXX seems to presuppose: בְּכָל־מְלָאכֶת.

22:8

עַל־כָּל־דְּבַר־פֶּשַׁע / κατὰ πᾶν ῥητὸν ἀδίκημα

The LXX has rather oddly understood דבר as adjectival, perhaps: עַל־כֹּל דָּבָר פֶּשַׁע.

ἀπωλείας τῆς ἐγκαλουμένης

See Anderson[9], *Greek Word Order in Contrast to Hebrew* on the attributive adjective.

כִּי־הוּא זֶה / ὅ τι οὖν ἂν ᾖ

The כִּי could be interpreted in two ways: 1) as a demonstrative particle suggesting a negative 'No, but!', 2) as a conjunction introducing a direct quotation. The LXX has a rather artificial interpretation of the Hebrew.

אֲשֶׁר יַרְשִׁיעֻן אֱלֹהִים / καὶ ὁ ἁλοὺς διὰ τοῦ θεοῦ

Although we might have expected: אֶת־אֲשֶׁר, it should be noted that the definite object particle is frequently omitted when the object precedes the verb. The LXX uses the aorist participle of the defective passive verb ἁλίσκομαι 'to be taken' (often in the sense 'to be convicted'). The LXX seems to be presupposing the use of Urim and Thumim. יַרְשִׁיעֻן appears to have been read as יֵרֵשׁ עַל. This reading does force the verb ירשׁ somewhat, which is also not otherwise found in the *Qal* passive.

יַרְשִׁיעֻן

See Jenni[2], 43-45 on the way in which a declarative *Hiphil* differs from a declarative *Piel*. The *Piel* has an estimative quality, while the *Hiphil* simply makes known or declares what is already reality. Jenni suggests 'allow to be guilty' for the *Hiphil* in such a context as here, although such a rendering is not exactly idiomatic English in this context.

22:10-13 (Hebr. 22:9-12)

Damage / theft to an animal in one's keeping

Translation

¹⁰ When someone gives his neighbour a donkey, a head of cattle or an animal from the flock or any animal for safekeeping and it dies or is wounded or is driven away while nobody is looking,

¹¹ let the oath of Y<small>HWH</small> come between the two of them whether he has not put forth his hand against the property of his neighbour and its owner will receive it (the oath) and he (the neighbour) will not make reparation.

¹² But if it really was stolen while in his possession, let him make reparation to its owner.

¹³ If it is indeed torn (by wild beasts), let him bring it as evidence, i.e. the animal torn (by a wild beast).¹¹⁴ He will not make reparation.

Commentary

Whilst the previous law dealt with inanimate goods given to someone for safekeeping, this law deals with the safekeeping of animals. In broad outline the same principle applies, that if the animal was damaged or driven away (i.e. stolen) and no blame attaches to the person who was looking after it, then no restitution is required. An oath may be required from the safekeeper to establish that no guilt rests with him (similarly, in the previous law, although that was not made specific, cf. Hebr. 6:16 and consult the introduction for more details on the use of this kind of oath). The implication is, of course, that if the

---

114. Alternatively: "If it is indeed torn (by wild beasts), let him bring him (the owner) to the torn animal."

safekeeper had been negligent, he would have to make restitution. If he can provide the evidence of an animal torn by wild beasts, no oath is required (v.13).[115] These legal principles were obviously quite old, given that Jacob complains that Laban did not respect them:

> *What was torn by wild beasts I did not bring to you. I bore the loss of it myself. From my hand you required it, whether stolen by day or stolen by night.* (Gen. 31:39)

The same regulation is probably in view in Amos 3:12.

> *Thus says the* LORD*: "As the shepherd rescues from the mouth of the lion two legs, or a piece of an ear, so shall the people of Israel who dwell in Samaria be rescued, with the corner of a couch and part of a bed."*

The problem of verse 12

A difficulty arises with verse 12. Why should the safekeeper pay restitution if the animal was stolen from him? And what is the difference between the 'theft' in this verse, which requires restitution and the 'driving away' from the previous verse, which does not require restitution? Two solutions are possible, both of which go back to ancient times.

Some interpreters argue that the safekeeping of an animal, because of the work involved, must have always been recompensed. In other words, that an animal would only be looked after for a fee, which places extra responsibility with the safekeeper and makes him responsible if the animal is stolen. On this interpretation verse 12 is concerned with theft by an individual, which ought to have been preventable and verse 11 concerns the activity of rustling for which the safekeeper cannot be held responsible. While possible, this solution does not really convince in the end. Nothing is said in the law about safekeeping for a fee and the context (coming right after the previous law on the safekeeping of inanimate goods) suggests that no fee or self-interest on the part of the safekeeper is present. In the second place, there is the question why

---

115. The LXX reads the Hebrew of v.12b differently so that instead of the safekeeper bringing the torn remains to the owner as evidence, he takes the owner to the torn remains.

the safekeeper would only be held responsible for theft, and not for an attack by a wild animal ('torn to shreds') etc.?

The second solution, which I believe to be the correct interpretation, would see this law as parallel to the previous law, dealing now with animate property. The point of verse 12, on this interpretation, is that when theft has definitely been established, the safekeeper should make restitution. The use of the Hebrew absolute infinitive for the 'theft' here should not be overlooked. I translate: "But if it <u>really was stolen</u> while in his possession ...", in other words if the thief has been caught and paid his penalty to the safekeeper (as in the previous law), then the safekeeper ought to provide restitution for the animal. The safekeeper would be able to keep the penalty payment for the theft (double for a donkey, 4 or 5 times for an animal from the herd or flock if not found intact).[116]

The consequences of perjury

It is interesting to note that the law for reparation sacrifices (cf. Lev. 6:1-7; Num. 5:5-8) provides regulations for those who have sworn a false oath in such cases as these laws. If a false oath has come to light a full restitution must be made with a penalty payment of twenty percent. The extra penalty (paid to the owner of the property) is given for the added sin of transgressing against God's holy name. Only after payment of the restitution and penalty may the priest accept the reparation offering and grant forgiveness in God's name.

---

116. As the previous law makes clear, if the safekeeper is found guilty of misappropriating the animal, his penalty would be a double recompense, regardless of the kind of animal.

Text

⁹ Ἐὰν δέ τις δῷ τῷ πλησίον ὑποζύγιον ἢ πρόβατον ἢ μόσχον ἢ πᾶν κτῆνος φυλάξαι, καὶ συντριβῇ ἢ τελευτήσῃ ἢ αἰχμάλωτον γένηται, καὶ μηδεὶς γνῷ, ¹⁰ ὅρκος ἔσται τοῦ θεοῦ ἀνὰ μέσον ἀμφοτέρων ἦ μὴν μὴ αὐτὸν πεπονηρεῦσθαι καθ' ὅλης τῆς παρακαταθήκης τοῦ πλησίον· καὶ οὕτως προσδέξεται ὁ κύριος αὐτοῦ, καὶ οὐ μὴ ἀποτείσει. ¹¹ ἐὰν δὲ κλαπῇ παρ' αὐτοῦ, ἀποτείσει τῷ κυρίῳ. ¹² ἐὰν δὲ θηριάλωτον γένηται, ἄξει αὐτὸν ἐπὶ τὴν θήραν, καὶ οὐκ ἀποτείσει.	כִּי־יִתֵּן אִישׁ אֶל־רֵעֵהוּ חֲמוֹר אוֹ־שׁוֹר אוֹ־שֶׂה וְכָל־בְּהֵמָה לִשְׁמֹר וּמֵת אוֹ־נִשְׁבַּר אוֹ־נִשְׁבָּה אֵין רֹאֶה: ¹⁰ שְׁבֻעַת יְהוָה תִּהְיֶה בֵּין שְׁנֵיהֶם אִם־לֹא שָׁלַח יָדוֹ בִּמְלֶאכֶת רֵעֵהוּ וְלָקַח בְּעָלָיו וְלֹא יְשַׁלֵּם: ¹¹ וְאִם־גָּנֹב יִגָּנֵב מֵעִמּוֹ יְשַׁלֵּם לִבְעָלָיו: ¹² אִם־טָרֹף יִטָּרֵף יְבִאֵהוּ עֵד הַטְּרֵפָה לֹא יְשַׁלֵּם:

שׁבה, *Qal* to deport; *Niph.* to be deported, taken captive טְרֵפָה, animal torn by wild beasts	θηριάλωτος, ον, caught by wild beasts (coinage)

22:9

כִּי־יִתֵּן אִישׁ / Ἐὰν δέ τις δῷ

On the question of a copulative, see the textual note to 21:37. Sam. Pent. reads וכי.

וּמֵת אוֹ־נִשְׁבָּה / καὶ συντριβῇ ἢ τελευτήσῃ ἢ αἰχμάλωτον γένηται

The variation in order in the LXX is repeated at 22:13, where the MT has the order of the LXX here, but misses the last option.

אֵין רֹאֶה / καὶ μηδεὶς γνῷ

Such an asyndetic clause (whether nominal as here, or verbal) is more common in Hebrew, cf. Joüon/Muraoka §159bc. The Greek has a copulative, both here and similarly in v.13.

22:10

שְׁבֻעַת יְהוָה / ὅρκος ἔσται τοῦ θεοῦ

Both the Greek word-order and the exchange of 'YHWH' for 'God' is curious, but probably an attempt to synchronise the use of 'God' with the LXX interpretation of v.8. This, of course, only reinforces the case for reading אֱלֹהִים as a plural referring to judges in v.8. The laws of the book of the covenant only use יהוה to refer to God, not אֱלֹהִים.

אִם־לֹא שָׁלַח יָדוֹ / ἦ μὴν μὴ κτλ.

See the note to 22:7.

בִּמְלֶאכֶת / καθ' ὅλης τῆς παρακαταθήκης

The LXX seems to presuppose: בְּכָל־מְלֶאכֶת.

וְלָקַח בְּעָלָיו / καὶ οὕτως προσδέξεται ὁ κύριος αὐτοῦ

Sc. אֶת־הַשְּׁבֻעָה. Note once again the plural of majesty with a singular verb. The masculine suffix must refer back to the animal in question. The LXX καὶ οὕτως προσδέξεται may represent וְלָכֵן יִקַּח.

22:11

יִגָּנֵב

This is the only example of the *Niphal* of גנב in the Old Testament. The verb 'to steal' is an accomplishment verb and thus does not appear in the *Hiphil*. The *Niphal* is thus derived from the *Qal*, expressing the middle voice of the ingressive *Qal*. We might paraphrase: 'But if, in fact, a stealing occurs with respect to it'. It is a fact that Hebrew tends to prefer the use of a medio-passive *Niphal* over the true *Qal* passive, which is quite rare in classical Hebrew. The *Niphal* is fitting here in that there is no interest in specifying an agent (which would require a true passive).

יְשַׁלֵּם

    The Sam. Pent. reads וֹשׁלם, that is, a perfect with the *waw* of apodosis, which may very well be correct. It should, however, be realised that the Sam. Pent. has updated and smoothed out the Hebrew text and adding a *waw* of apodosis belongs to this editorial process. In this instance, however, it is quite possible that an original *waw* was mistaken for a *yod*.

22:11-12

אִם : לִבְעָלָיו / τῷ κυρίῳ. ἐὰν δὲ

    The suffix in the MT has been treated as a copulative by the LXX.

22:12

יְבִאֵהוּ עֵד הַטְּרֵפָה / ἄξει αὐτὸν ἐπὶ τὴν θήραν

    An additional complement (actually a fem. noun) explains the masculine object suffix (referring to the animal) attached to the verb: 'he shall bring it as a witness, i.e. the torn thing'. Note that the noun עֵד is more often used not only of a human witness, but also of objects used as evidence. The LXX has pointed עֵד as עַד and either read הַטֶּרֶף for הַטְּרֵפָה or given it an identical meaning. The idea is then that the safekeeper take the owner to see the prey, that is, his torn animal. Note that the *Naqdanim* have made הַטְּרֵפָה an accusative of respect to the final clause by placing an *athnach* under עֵד.

לֹא יְשַׁלֵּם / καὶ οὐκ ἀποτείσει

    Along with the different text read by the LXX in the previous words is an extra *waw*, also present in the Sam. Pent.

22:14-15 (Hebr. 22:13-14)

Damage to an animal borrowed or hired

Translation

[14] And when someone borrows (an animal) from his neighbour and it is wounded or dies while its owner is not with it[117], he shall surely make reparation.

[15] If its owner was with it he will not make reparation, if it was hired it went (back) for its hire-price.

Commentary

The previous two laws concerned property given for safekeeping. The safekeeper was doing the owner of the property a favour. In this case it is the owner of the property who is doing a favour to another person. His property has been borrowed so that the borrower can make use of it. Any damage to the property must be recompensed, unless the owner was also with it at the time of the damage. In the latter case the owner remains responsible for the use of his own property. If the property was not borrowed, but hired, then there is no requirement of restitution as the risk of damage was calculated in the hire. Presumably damage through gross negligence or deliberate misuse would be a different story. Although not mentioned specifically, the kinds of damage which may incur to the property show that an animal is in view. Indeed, draft animals being expensive both in capital cost and maintenance would not have been owned by everyone. Nor was this necessary, given that the variability of the winter rains from year to year make a system of staggered ploughing and sowing a necessity to farmers in the highlands

---

117. Alternatively: 'its owner is not with him (i.e. the borrower)'. The same possibility applies to v.15.

of Canaan. There was therefore plenty of time to make good use of a limited number of draft animals.[118]

The Septuagint interprets the last phrase concerned with hire differently than most translations. Although the 'hired thing' is normally interpreted as the animal, it is here the hired day-labourer. In this case, the point is that if a day-labourer has borrowed an animal from his employer in order to do his work, then any damage to the animal will be docked from his pay. On this interpretation we are left in the dark as to what would happen if the animal was worth more than his day's wage.

---

118   Hopkins, 215-17.

Text

¹³ Ἐὰν δὲ αἰτήσῃ τις παρὰ τοῦ πλησίον, καὶ συντριβῇ ἢ ἀποθάνῃ, ὁ δὲ κύριος μὴ ᾖ μετ' αὐτοῦ, ἀποτείσει· ¹⁴ ἐὰν δὲ ὁ κύριος ᾖ μετ' αὐτοῦ, οὐκ ἀποτείσει· ἐὰν δὲ μισθωτὸς ᾖ, ἔσται αὐτῷ ἀντὶ τοῦ μισθοῦ αὐτοῦ.	וְכִי־יִשְׁאַל אִישׁ מֵעִם רֵעֵהוּ וְנִשְׁבַּר אוֹ־מֵת בְּעָלָיו אֵין־עִמּוֹ שַׁלֵּם יְשַׁלֵּם: ¹⁴ אִם־בְּעָלָיו עִמּוֹ לֹא יְשַׁלֵּם אִם־שָׂכִיר הוּא בָּא בִּשְׂכָרוֹ:

שָׂכִיר, hireling, day-labourer (human or animal)	שָׂכָר, wages

22:13

בְּעָלָיו / ὁ δὲ κύριος

Note the plural of majesty. The LXX appears to have read וּבְעָלָיו.

שַׁלֵּם יְשַׁלֵּם / ἀποτείσει

As more often with this verb, the LXX appears not to have read the absolute infinitive.

22:14

אִם־שָׂכִיר / ἐὰν δὲ μισθωτὸς ᾖ κτλ.

For the interpretation of the LXX here, see the main commentary. For the addition of δέ, see the textual note to 21:4.

הוּא בָּא / ἔσται αὐτῷ

The LXX has read הוא לו. The Sam. Pent. read ובא הוא, that is, a *waw* of apodosis.

22:16-17 (Hebr. 22:15-16)

CASE LAWS
LAWS WITH PENAL SANCTIONS:
4. OTHER LAWS

Defilement of a man's virgin daughter

Translation

[16] And when someone entices a virgin who is not betrothed and lies with her, he shall surely make a bridal payment for her to be a wife for himself.

[17] If her father flatly refuses and is unwilling to give her to him, he shall weigh out silver according to the bridal payment of virgins.

Commentary

This law is paralleled in Deuteronomy 22:28-29 as follows:

> Deut. 22:28-29. *When someone finds a young virgin who is not betrothed and seizes her and lies with her and they are discovered, then the man lying with her shall give to the father of the young woman fifty silver shekels and she shall be his wife because he has humbled her. He may not divorce her all his days.* (my translation)

Both of these laws speak about sex before marriage with a virgin girl. The law of Deuteronomy is set within a larger section dealing with sexual matters. Immediately prior to it, a law is given with respect to a man who lies with a betrothed woman. In that case a distinction is made between rape and consenting sexual activity. Such a distinction does not apply to lying with a virgin. However, the Book of the Covenant has already made it clear that a father may refuse to allow his daughter to marry in such a case. Given that in ancient Israel a raped girl would likely never again have the opportunity to marry, there was often a strong case for the social and legal protection of marriage in such a situation. Tamar having been raped by Amnon insists that he marry her (2 Sam. 13) and Jacob too arranged for his raped daughter Dinah to be married to Shechem (Gen. 34).

We should, however, not be distracted from the main point, namely, that these laws show us that pre-marital sexual activity is reserved by the Lord for the bond of marriage and that when this occurs with a non-married girl it places an obligation on the male perpetrator to marry her. The question of whether or not the girl has become pregnant has no bearing on this obligation. God has restricted physical unity to marriage. A fine is to be paid to the father of the girl, stipulated in Deuteronomy at 50 shekels of silver. This fine is called 'the bride-price' in the ESV of Exodus 22, but the translation can be confusing for it might appear that a dowry is meant. That is not the case.

Dowry versus bridal payment

It certainly was, and is, an Eastern custom for a dowry to be paid when a daughter is given away in marriage. We learn from the Bible that this was also the practice in Israel. We see, for example, both in 1 Kings 9:16 and Micah 1:13-14 the custom of paying a dowry to the girl. But, and this is particularly noteworthy, Gods law says nothing about this practice at all. Dowries are nowhere regulated in the Bible. The only thing we read in this regard is that when there has been sexual intercourse before marriage a fine of 50 shekels of silver must be paid to the father of the girl. The term used (*mōhar*) is found only three times in Scripture: here in this law, in Genesis 34:12 of the fine Hamor offers to pay after his son raped Jacob's daughter, and 1 Samuel 18:25 of the payment Saul requires of David for marrying his daughter. This last usage suggests that the payment made is related to the purchase of a slave-girl to be one's wife (see the commentary at Exod. 21:7-11). By stealing a girl's virginity a man has, as it were, taken the girl to be his wife. He must therefore make a bridal payment (*mōhar*). But in this case the payment takes the form of a punishment both in the amount due and in the fact that the father is at liberty to take the money and keep his daughter from marrying him as well.

When we consider that the average annual salary for a labourer in Moses' time was ten silver shekels, we may conclude that such a fine was roughly equivalent to five years wages![119] If such an amount could not be raised the only solution would be debt-slavery. Once again we may compare the value given to various sexes and ages in Leviticus 27:1-7 (as was done in the exposition of Exod. 21:28-32). We then see that 50 shekels is an amount far above the working value of the girl concerned.

Male 20-60 yrs	50 silver shekels
Female 20-60 yrs	30 silver shekels
Male 5-20 yrs	20 silver shekels
Female 5-20 yrs	10 silver shekels
Male 1 mth – 5 yrs	5 silver shekels
Female 1 mth – 5 yrs	3 silver shekels

The payment was a punishment and shows that this sin is not small in God's eyes. Stealing the gifts of marriage in advance has clear consequences (cf. 1 Cor. 6:18-20).

Marriage not compulsory

Along with the requirement to marry in such circumstances, the law also provides a safety measure. The father of the girl (as head of the family) has the right to refuse permission for such a marriage.[120] This

---

119. See De Vaux, 76. This comparison can only give a relative impression of the size of the fine. The position of a labourer in Old Testament society cannot be identified with that of today. Of interest is that the Jews never adjusted this specified amount for inflation. By the time of the New Testament 1 shekel was considered to be a normal *daily* wage for a day labourer (cf. Matt. 20:2).

120. It is not my intention to suggest that the mother has no role to play (see Prov. 6:20). In our society it would be normal (and also good) that parents

is for the girl's own protection, particularly in the case of rape. Even without a suggestion of rape, it is still possible that the boy or man is not at all suited for the girl. This is something that the father of the girl must determine. Sex before marriage does not automatically lead to a forced marriage. However, we must remember that the participants have stolen in advance what rightly belongs only to marriage. Whether or not the marriage goes ahead, the fine must still be paid. This situation is aptly mirrored in what happened after the rape of Jacob's daughter Dinah by Shechem. Shechem freely agrees to pay whatever bridal payment (*mōhar*) is imposed upon him. But at the same time he pleads to be able to take Dinah as his wife as well.

> "*Ask me for as great a bride-price and gift as you will, and I will give whatever you say to me. Only give me the young woman to be my wife.*" (Gen. 34:12)

It is to be noted that the Bible speaks from the position that a father gives his daughter away to her husband. It is important that the father grant permission for his daughter to marry.[121] The Bible clearly speaks (with reference to the father) of *giving in marriage* (if a woman were to marry for a second time she would do so independently, 1 Cor. 7:39). Through the formation of a new marriage-bond the authority of the parents comes to a definitive end. The wording of Genesis 2:24 is quite illustrative at this point:

> *Therefore a man shall leave his father and his mother and hold fast to his wife, and they shall become one flesh.*

---

discuss such matters together. The father, as head, will provide leadership and bear the final responsibility (just as Adam – not Eve – had to bear the final responsibility for the fall into sin).

121. Christian tradition still has the practice of a young man asking permission from the father of his fiancée to take her hand in marriage. This is not just a polite, laudable practice, but a tradition with a Biblical foundation. It is not necessarily wrong for a boy and a girl to get to know one another before they marry, but the permission to marry given by the parents of the girl is a Biblical requirement. For this reason it is also appropriate to ask the father of a girl for permission to court her. Such a request shows recognition of the fact that the girl being courted is not to be treated as a free agent. She remains under the authority of her parents. Maltreatment of her or sexual activity with her, whether or not she consents, is sin against her parents.

The book of Genesis steps outside of the narrative for a moment and draws a conclusion for the reader. It is significant that we are told that the 'man' leaves his parents to cleave to his wife. We are not told that the girl leaves her parents. In fact, in biblical terms, she does not *leave* them, but she is *given* by them to her new husband.

All of this shows that when sex has occurred before marriage, the boy or man has certain responsibilities over against the father of the girl. It is the father's duty to give his daughter away in marriage, regardless of her age. The sin must also be humbly confessed to the father.[122] The seriousness of the sin is expressed by the size of the fine. If the father consents to the obligation to marry, the girl, whose virginity has definitively been lost, becomes his responsibility and under his care.

Yet one more consequence follows for the newly married couple. Where sexual intercourse has occurred before marriage, God ordains in Deuteronomy 22:29 that the couple may never divorce. Such a marriage may never be annulled. Herein a certain protection is again afforded to the girl. She may never be abandoned. Her husband will always be responsible for her well-being, even if they should come upon difficult times in which it is necessary to separate. He will, as long as he lives, be responsible for her protection and support.

---

122. Although Deut. 22:28 speaks of two people who are 'found' out, God expects us, if we have genuine repentance for our sin, to come forward and confess it. Repentance involves humbly accepting the punishment and consequences of our sins. Any attempt to hide our sins in order to circumvent our biblical responsibilities shows a lack of repentance and effectively blocks any private prayer for forgiveness.

Text

¹⁵ Ἐὰν δὲ ἀπατήσῃ τις παρθένον ἀμνήστευτον, καὶ κοιμηθῇ μετ' αὐτῆς, φερνῇ φερνιεῖ αὐτὴν αὐτῷ γυναῖκα. ¹⁶ ἐὰν δὲ ἀνανεύων ἀνανεύσῃ καὶ μὴ βούληται ὁ πατὴρ αὐτῆς δοῦναι αὐτὴν αὐτῷ γυναῖκα, ἀργύριον ἀποτείσει τῷ πατρὶ καθ' ὅσον ἐστὶν ἡ φερνὴ τῶν παρθένων.	וְכִי־יְפַתֶּה אִישׁ בְּתוּלָה אֲשֶׁר לֹא־אֹרָשָׂה וְשָׁכַב עִמָּהּ מָהֹר יִמְהָרֶנָּה לּוֹ לְאִשָּׁה: ¹⁶ אִם־מָאֵן יְמָאֵן אָבִיהָ לְתִתָּהּ לוֹ כֶּסֶף יִשְׁקֹל כְּמֹהַר הַבְּתוּלֹת:

פתה, *Qal* to be simple, gullible; *Piel* entice, allure	φερνή, ἡ, bridal gift, dowry
בְּתוּלָה, virgin	φερνίζω, to give a bridal gift
אָרַשׂ, *Piel* to betroth, *Pual* to become betrothed	ἀνανεύω, to throw the head back in token of denial
מֹהַר, bride-price	

22:15

אֹרָשָׂה

Note the compensatory lengthening (with an *aleph*) of the short *u* of the *Pual* into a long *o* (Davidson, §7.7a). The lengthened second syllable is pausal.

מָהֹר יִמְהָרֶנָּה לּוֹ לְאִשָּׁה / φερνῇ φερνιεῖ αὐτὴν αὐτῷ γυναῖκα

The verb מהר in this sense is only used here. It is a denominative based on the noun מֹהַר, which itself is only used three times (Gen. 34:12; Exod. 22:16; 1 Sam. 18:25). It is clearly not a dowry, but rather an indemnity to the family. The מֹהַר is what Shechem offers to Jacob to take Dinah (whom he raped) as his wife. It is also what Saul alludes to when he makes David pay 100 foreskins of the Philistines for taking his daughter as wife. We might translate rather literally: "he shall surely make a bride-payment for her to be a wife for himself." The LXX with its very literal translation is unclear in its interpretation.

Note the *daghesh forte conjunctivum* in לּוֹ helping the enunciation of the ל after a ה.

22:16

אִם־מָאֵן יְמָאֵן אָבִיהָ / ἐὰν δὲ ἀνανεύων ἀνανεύσῃ καὶ μὴ βούληται ὁ πατὴρ αὐτῆς

The LXX presupposes a longer text with וְלֹא יֹאבֶה preceding אָבִיהָ. It would seem more probable that the longer text was accidentally omitted by haplography than that it was purposely added. For the addition of δέ after ἐάν, see the textual note to 21:4. The Sam. Pent. reads ואם.

לְתִתָּהּ לוֹ / δοῦναι αὐτὴν αὐτῷ γυναῖκα

Reflecting v.15, the LXX adds the equivalent of לְאִשָּׁה.

כֶּסֶף יִשְׁקֹל / ἀργύριον ἀποτείσει τῷ πατρὶ

The LXX may have read כֶּסֶף יְשַׁלֵּם לָאָב.

22:18 (Hebr. 22:17)

Death penalty for a sorceress

Translation

¹⁸ You shall not let a sorceress live.

Commentary

Sorcery carries a mandatory death penalty, as is clear from the striking formulation that a sorceress is not to be left alive. It becomes immediately clear that Saul transgressed this law when he merely banished sorcerers from the holy land (1 Sam. 28:3). Sorcery is an extreme form of public idolatry which, by its very nature, induces others to follow. Idolatry in any form could not be tolerated in a land, which was dedicated as 'holy' to God. Although it is clear from the Mosaic law that there were also male practitioners of sorcery, it would appear that the most danger came from women. Further laws against sorcery can be found in Leviticus 19:31; 20:6, 27 and Deuteronomy 18:9-14. The reader should also consult 1 Samuel 28 (Saul and the medium at Endor); 2 Kings 9:21-26 (Jezebel); 21:6 (cf. 2 Chr. 33:6, Manasseh); Isaiah 47:9; Jeremiah 27:8-11; Micah 5:10-15; Nahum 3:1-4 and Malachi 3:5. The case of king Saul is particularly interesting in that we are told that he only visited a medium after having failed in all the various ways in inquiring of YHWH, who did not answer him. These ways are listed as dreams, Urim and prophets (1 Sam. 28:6). From our perspective we may recall the words of Hebrews 1:1-2a "Long ago, at many times and in many ways, God spoke to our fathers by the prophets, but in these last days he has spoken to us by his Son".

Certain other capital crimes should probably also be considered as requiring a mandatory death penalty. When we take into account the fact that it was left to the accuser (or plaintiff) to choose for a substitutionary fine or not, we may conclude that where there is no direct plaintiff the prescribed punishment must be executed. This would certainly be the case for crimes in which God himself was the plaintiff, that is, crimes which were clearly committed against God such as public blasphemy (Lev. 24:10ff; cf. Heid.Cat. Q/A 100) and working on the Sabbath (Exod. 31:15).

Text

¹⁷ Φαρμακοὺς οὐ περιποιήσετε.	מְכַשֵּׁפָה לֹא תְחַיֶּה׃

כשׁף, *Piel* to practise sorcery חיה, *Qal* to be/stay alive, *Piel* to let live	περιποιέω, keep safe, preserve

22:17

מְכַשֵּׁפָה לֹא תְחַיֶּה / Φαρμακοὺς οὐ περιποιήσετε

The LXX reads מְכַשְּׁפִים. This text is the only place where the feminine participle 'sorceress' is used with this verb-form. The LXX may also have read the plural verb form: תְּחַיּוּ(ן).

The term φαρμακός (or perhaps better φάρμακος) appears only in Jewish and Christian writings (e.g. LXX, NT in Rev.) in the sense of sorcery. It obviously originates in a sorcerer's use of drugs or herbs in creating magic potions. The second century AD grammarian Herodian, however, distinguishes φαρμακός from φάρμακος as follows (which suggests that the word was also known in regular Greek): <φαρμακός> ὁ ἐπὶ καθαρμῷ τῆς πόλεως τελευτῶν, <φάρμακος> δὲ ὁ γόης (*De prosodia catholica*, bk.6; vol.1, p.150 ed. Lentz).

Words for Sorcery

There are various words used for sorcery (magic) and soothsaying (interpreting signs and omens) in Hebrew. Unfortunately, we are no longer able to precisely determine distinctions in meaning and their varied use suggests that they may not ever have been all that precise anyway.

כשׁף *Piel* 'to practise sorcery'. The root has the same meaning in Akkadian and Ugaritic. It is a denominative verb and normally only used in Hebrew as a participle indicating the profession of sorcerer or soothsayer. It is only once used as a finite verb (of king Manasseh, 2 Chron. 33:6). It is used for both the practice of magic as well as interpreting signs (soothsaying).

כֶּשֶׁף 'sorcery'. The noun is only used in the plural.

כַּשָּׁף 'sorcerer' (*hapax* in Jer. 27:9)

ענן *Poel*[123] 'to practise soothsaying', may be a denominative of עָנָן (clouds) and so 'to interpret the clouds'. The participle מְעוֹנֵן is used of the profession.

נחשׁ *Piel* 'to practise soothsaying'. It is unclear whether or not the word for 'snake' (נָחָשׁ) is etymologically related. The participle מְנַחֵשׁ is used of the profession.

נַחַשׁ 'magic curse', 'omen'

קסם 'to practice soothsaying'

קֶסֶם 'prediction' (by interpretation of signs or oracles)

שׁחר *Piel* used generally 'to be on the lookout for', but also in the *Qal* part. as 'sorcerer' in Isa. 47.

Two nouns are only used for foreign sorcerers or soothsayers:

אַשָּׁף conjurer (i.e. one who uses magic) = Aramaic loanword used in Daniel (1:20; 2:2)

חַרְטֹם soothsayer priests, whether Egyptian or Babylonian. There is no certain derivation.

---

123. The *Poel* is, next to the *Piel*, a common factitive form for double *'Ayin* verbs.

22:19 (Hebr. 22:18)

Death penalty for bestiality

Translation

¹⁹ Everyone who lies with an animal shall surely be killed.

Commentary

Another mandatory death penalty (there being no opportunity for the accuser to bargain for a fine) is provided for sex with an animal. This law applies to both male and female transgressors (cf. Lev. 18:23; 20:16 and Deut. 27:21). Interestingly, Leviticus 20:16 (concerning a woman with a male animal) requires the death of both the person and the animal.

Text

| ¹⁸ Πᾶν κοιμώμενον μετὰ κτήνους, θανάτῳ ἀποκτενεῖτε αὐτούς. | כָּל־שֹׁכֵב עִם־בְּהֵמָה מוֹת יוּמָת׃ |

| κοιμάω, to put to sleep; *Mid./Pass.* to fall asleep, lie down |

22:18

Πᾶν κοιμώμενον

    We should have expected πάντα. Is this a deliberate snub on someone committing bestiality? Thackeray (173-75), however, notes that this use of the neuter πᾶν for the masculine occurs more frequently in the LXX and provides a detailed discussion.

מוֹת יוּמָת / θανάτῳ ἀποκτενεῖτε αὐτούς

    The LXX appears to have read: מוֹת תְּמִיתוּם, retaining the second person form common to this section of the book of the covenant.

22:20-21 (Hebr. 22:19-20)

THE BAN

The ban for sacrifice to other gods, but a sojourner not to be oppressed

Translation

[20] He who sacrifices to the gods, except to Y<small>HWH</small> alone, will be under the ban.

[21] But you shall not oppress a sojourner nor exert pressure on him for you were sojourners in the land of Egypt.

Commentary

Sacrifice is an act of worship and in Israel the only permissible worship was that dedicated to Y<small>HWH</small>, the covenant God. It is important to understand that sacrifice was the acceptable way of actually *communicating* with God. In other words, sacrifice made it possible to speak with God in prayer. Later, the morning and evening sacrifices in the tabernacle / temple would enable Israelites not physically present to pray to God by extending their hands towards the sanctuary at these times of sacrifice. Solomon makes this explicit in his dedicatory prayer as follows:

> [44] "If your people go out to battle against their enemy, by whatever way you shall send them, and they pray to the L<small>ORD</small> toward the city that you have chosen and the house that I have built for your name, [45] then hear in heaven their prayer and their plea, and maintain

their cause. ⁴⁶ "If they sin against you—for there is no one who does not sin—and you are angry with them and give them to an enemy, so that they are carried away captive to the land of the enemy, far off or near, ⁴⁷ yet if they turn their heart in the land to which they have been carried captive, and repent and plead with you in the land of their captors, saying, 'We have sinned and have acted perversely and wickedly,' ⁴⁸ if they repent with all their heart and with all their soul in the land of their enemies, who carried them captive, and pray to you toward their land, which you gave to their fathers, the city that you have chosen, and the house that I have built for your name, ⁴⁹ then hear in heaven your dwelling place their prayer and their plea, and maintain their cause ⁵⁰ and forgive your people who have sinned against you, and all their transgressions that they have committed against you, and grant them compassion in the sight of those who carried them captive, that they may have compassion on them ... " (1 Kgs 8:44-50)

In the time of the Exodus, however, an altar needed to be built and personal animals sacrificed to enable prayer to God. Sacrifice was also more than just provision for communicating with God. It was the gifting of sacrificial animals bred domestically within the promised land. Because this promised land was YHWH's land, animals dedicated to sacrifice within this land were to be considered his *property* and thus 'holy'.

The law is spoken to those who desire to communicate with YHWH. Foreigners, who did not worship YHWH, were not compelled to convert. They could continue living in Israel as long as they did not openly offer sacrifice to a foreign god.

This law forms a kind of transition from the penal code. The ban is not a civil, but a religious punishment. It is, however, arguably the most serious punishment possible.[124] The ban was the punishment enacted when God's property (ritually designated 'holy') was stolen. In the case described by this law, all sacrificial animals within the holy land

---

124. The NKJV describes the consequences of the ban with its translation "shall be utterly destroyed", but omits reference to the technical terminology used.

are to be considered his property and therefore may not be given to another deity.[125]

The history of Achan in Joshua 7 shows how the ban was to be carried out. The person and all his belongings, including wife and children, were to be killed and then burned with fire. That which is put under the ban becomes a whole burnt offering to YHWH (cf. Deut. 13:15-17). In this way, that which belongs to YHWH may not be taken from him and given to another god. He claims it back for himself as a burnt offering. The ban may be viewed as a precursor of the punishment to be meted out upon the whole sinful world (which ultimately belongs to the creator) upon the last day when the earth and its works will be burnt up (cf. 2 Pet. 3:10-13). Leviticus 27:28-29 adds that the ban is a mandatory penalty which does not allow for redemption.[126]

In Deuteronomy 13 and 17:2-5 stoning is stipulated as the manner of punishment for an individual Israelite who serves, or entices others to serve, other gods. The ban only applies when God's property is stolen. Deuteronomy 13:15-17 does mention the ban with regard to the possibility that an entire city publicly engages in idolatry. Clearly the law presumes that when a city has gone over to the service of another god (or gods), sacrifices will have taken place.

The inhabitants of Canaan were to be eradicated and placed under the ban because YHWH had claimed that land for himself as holy and therefore all those guilty of idolatry within its territories were to be prosecuted according to this law (cf. Exod. 34:12-16; Deut. 20:16-18). They had stolen God's land. In addition, God indicated that his patience with the extreme sinfulness of the Canaanites had reached its end (cf. Gen. 15:16). The fact that God had the Israelites execute

---

125. It is interesting to compare the *codex Hammurabi* in this respect. Stealing from a god is punished by the requirement to pay back what was stolen thirtyfold (§8).

126. This law raises the question as to the supposed leniency towards those Israelites who were sacrificing animals to goat demons in the wilderness (Lev. 17:7). There is insufficient information to say much about this, but it is probable that God gave the warning and change in sacrificial law concerning this matter because he knew what was going on. The perpetrators themselves will have done this secretly and may have escaped notice and thus prosecution.

this ban on his behalf became a kind of test of faith. The Israelites were to have none of the usual profits of plunder from this holy war. Everything was to be dedicated to God.

The ban (Hebrew *cherem*) was translated in the Septuagint as *anathema* (ἀνάθεμα), a term which in normal Greek would refer to a votive offering, but among the Jews came to refer to the 'ban'. According to rabbinical sources, the synagogues came to use the concept of placing someone under the 'ban' (*cherem*) for the most severe form of excommunication.[127] A person who had been placed 'under the ban' had to be shunned more completely than someone who had been placed under temporary ostracism (a penalty imposed up to a maximum of 60 days). A person under the ban was not admitted to schooling and one was not to have economic profit from him (no business dealings). The sources are silent with respect to the length of the ban and the possibility of lifting it. It is, however, probable that such a ban was for an undetermined length of time, but that upon repentance it could be lifted.

The apostle Paul (using the term *anathema* / ἀνάθεμα) places the Judaisers, who preached a Gospel of works, under the ban in Galatians 1:8-9. In the same letter he distinguishes the ban from the concept of curse (*katara* / κατάρα) – a prayer that God punish someone (see Gal. 3:10). Generally speaking, those who do not love the Lord Jesus are also to be placed under the ban (1 Cor. 16:22), a sentence tantamount, in this period, to excommunication (cf. Rom. 9:3). In 1 Corinthians 12:3 Paul seems to allude to the fact that the Corinthian Jews had placed Jesus under the ban, when he says:

> Therefore I want you to understand that no one speaking in the Spirit of God ever says "Jesus is accursed (anathema / ἀνάθεμα)!" and no one can say "Jesus is Lord" except in the Holy Spirit.

Sojourners

The ban for sacrificing to any god other than Y$_{HWH}$ is immediately followed by the command not to oppress a stranger in the land. It is connected to the previous verse in the form of a circumstantial clause.

---

127. See "Der Synagogenbann" in Strack & Billerbeck, vol.4.1, 293-333.

A circumstantial clause, which is indicated in Hebrew by a particular word order, gives expression to a circumstance directly related to what has just been said. Thus, although sacrificing to other gods in Israel is a serious offence, this fact gives no warrant for oppressing sojourners, who more often than not were not worshippers of Yʜᴡʜ. This law is more or less repeated at 23:9. It is also found at Leviticus 19:33-34 with the same motivation and the additional command to love the sojourner as oneself. The law is also reflected in Deuteronomy 10:18-19 (showing love to the sojourner by giving him food and clothing); 24:17 and 27:19 (no perversion of justice for a sojourner). Malachi 3:5 speaks of Yʜᴡʜ being a witness against those who turn aside the justice due to a sojourner.

A 'sojourner' (*gēr* / גֵּר) was a person who had left his own village or city, usually because of war, famine or some other calamity, and settled in another place where he had limited citizen's rights. We might today call him a 'refugee'. It ought to be remembered that no sojourner could own permanent land in Israel as the land belonged to the various families and reverted back at the year of Jubilee. However, this does not mean that a sojourner could not rent land for a specified period.

It is quite obvious that a sojourner was an easy target for oppression. The Israelites are therefore reminded that they were once in the same precarious position. It would seem to be implied that they ought not to engage in the same sin of oppression as the Egyptians did when pressing them into slavery.

Text

[19] Ὁ θυσιάζων θεοῖς ἐξολεθρευθήσεται πλὴν κυρίῳ μόνῳ. [20] Καὶ προσήλυτον οὐ κακώσετε οὐδὲ μὴ θλίψητε αὐτόν· ἦτε γὰρ προσήλυτοι ἐν γῇ Αἰγύπτῳ.	זֹבֵחַ לָאֱלֹהִים יָחֳרָם בִּלְתִּי לַיהוָה לְבַדּוֹ: [20] וְגֵר לֹא־תוֹנֶה וְלֹא תִלְחָצֶנּוּ כִּי־גֵרִים הֱיִיתֶם בְּאֶרֶץ מִצְרָיִם:

| בִּלְתִּי, not, excluding, without
 ינה, *Hiph.* to afflict, oppress | לחץ, *Qal* to exert pressure, oppress |

22:19

זֹבֵחַ / Ὁ θυσιάζων

The LXX may have read: הַזֹּבֵחַ.

יַחֲרָם

Note the use of a helping vowel under the guttural ח, instead of a silent *shewa* (Davidson, §7.5).

22:20

וְגֵר / Καὶ προσήλυτον

The word-order here (conjunction + noun instead of verb) may be construed as a circumstantial clause, which shows that this verse should be connected to the preceding. While only Y<small>HWH</small> is to be worshipped in Israel, this does not give the Israelites the right to oppress strangers who may not be converts. By the first century BC these terms (both in Hebrew and Greek) had come to refer to a convert to Judaism.

הֱיִיתֶם ... תִּלְחָצֶנּוּ ... תוֹנֶה / κακώσετε ... θλίψητε ..., ἦτε

The variation in number (sing., sing., plural) in Hebrew is curious (although such variation is common in Deuteronomy). The LXX and Sam. Pent. read the whole verse as second person plurals (... תּוֹנוּ תִלְחָצֻהוּ).

LAWS WITHOUT SANCTIONS

As noted in the introduction, the following laws concern matters to which no sanctions are attached. As such they are not legally enforceable by a court of law. They describe the kind of *righteousness* (a relational term in Hebrew, see the introduction) which God expects of his covenant people.

22:22-24 (Hebr. 22:21-23)

Don't afflict widows or orphans

Translation

²² You shall not afflict any widow or fatherless child,

²³ but if you indeed afflict him, surely if he cries out to me I will certainly hear his cry

²⁴ and my nose will become hot (in anger) and I will kill you with a sword[128] and your wives will become widows and your children will become fatherless.

Commentary

If sojourners, having limited rights in society, were the most vulnerable, widows and orphans were not far behind. We should realise that the term 'orphan' refers to children without a father as Lamentations 5:3 makes clear:

> We have become orphans, fatherless; our mothers are like widows.

Children without a father were in a financially perilous position. Widows could easily be oppressed such that their children would have

---

128. I.e. 'in battle'.

to be sold into slavery. The story of the widow in 2 Kings 4:1 who was in danger of losing her sons as slaves to creditors would not have been all that unusual. In fact, Nehemiah 5:5 refers to the same plight in his criticism of the people in his own day:

> *Now our flesh is as the flesh of our brothers, our children are as their children. Yet we are forcing our sons and our daughters to be slaves, and some of our daughters have already been enslaved, but it is not in our power to help it, for other men have our fields and our vineyards.*

The kind of concern which other laws applied to the poor in general would apply particularly to widows and orphans (cf. Deut. 15:9, a warning to ensure the release of debts in the seventh year, Deut. 24:15 paying wages on the day of work done).

The point of the law is that widows and orphans were often not able to find justice through the legal system. Creditors were legally within their rights to demand payment and even to enforce sale of children to pay off a debt (2 Kgs 4). That which is *legally* correct is, however, not necessarily *righteous* (see the introduction). God here promises that he, as the great King, will ensure that their justice is served – and his justice may turn out worse for the offender than that of a human court. God promises to be a 'father' for orphans (Ps. 68:5). The afflicted who have no recourse to justice in an earthly court may appeal to him directly in prayer. The cry of the poor who are oppressed is mentioned by Elihu in Job 34:28. A good example of the kind of prayer for vengeance from the widow or orphan which is implied by this law may be found in Psalm 109.

Text

| ²¹ πᾶσαν χήραν καὶ ὀρφανὸν οὐ κακώσετε· ²² ἐὰν δὲ κακίᾳ κακώσητε αὐτούς, καὶ κεκράξαντες καταβοήσωσι πρός με, ἀκοῇ εἰσακούσομαι τῆς φωνῆς αὐτῶν, ²³ καὶ ὀργισθήσομαι θυμῷ, καὶ ἀποκτενῶ ὑμᾶς μαχαίρᾳ, καὶ ἔσονται αἱ γυναῖκες ὑμῶν χῆραι, καὶ τὰ παιδία ὑμῶν ὀρφανά. | ²²כָּל־אַלְמָנָה וְיָתוֹם לֹא תְעַנּוּן: אִם־עַנֵּה תְעַנֶּה אֹתוֹ כִּי אִם־צָעֹק ²³ יִצְעַק אֵלַי שָׁמֹעַ אֶשְׁמַע צַעֲקָתוֹ: וְחָרָה אַפִּי וְהָרַגְתִּי אֶתְכֶם בֶּחָרֶב וְהָיוּ נְשֵׁיכֶם אַלְמָנוֹת וּבְנֵיכֶם יְתֹמִים: |

| יָתוֹם, fatherless orphan | εἰσακούω, to yield to |

22:21b-22a

תְּעַנֶּה אִם־עַנֵּה תְעַנּוּן: / κακώσετε, ἐὰν δὲ κακίᾳ κακώσητε

The LXX may have read וְאִם־עַנֵּה תְעַנּוּ תְעַנּוּ, but see the textual note to 21:4. The Sam. Pent. reads תענו: כי אם ענה תענו.

22:22

κεκράξαντες

The reduplicated 1ˢᵗ aorist is also found in the NT (Acts 24:21).

אֶשְׁמַע צַעֲקָתוֹ / εἰσακούσομαι τῆς φωνῆς αὐτῶν

Note the omission of אֶת־, which is not always readily explainable, although if it is lacking with a direct object placed after its verb, there are generally no words intervening between verb and object. The verb εἰσακούω is LXX vocabulary. It is not common outside the LXX, not even in the New Testament. Luke uses this verb for the language of angels only.

The LXX has plural pronouns for the singulars of the MT referring to the objects of affliction in this verse..

22:25 (Hebr. 22:24)

No interest on loans to the poor

Translation

²⁵ If it is money that you lend your poor brother, you will not be to him as one who lends at interest. You shall not lay interest upon him.

Commentary

The point of this law is that loans made to poor Israelites ought not to be viewed as commercial contracts. More literally, when a person lends *money* to the poor, he is not to be as "one lending on a contractual basis" (i.e. in Hebrew a *nōsheh* / נֹשֶׁה). No interest is to be exacted. The Hebrew text emphasises that it is indeed a lending of money (as opposed to animals, for example) that this law is concerned with. Leviticus 25:35-38 echoes this law amidst a larger section on dealing with the poor. It adds that interest may not be charged on food either. A generation later Deuteronomy 23:19-20 echoes the same concern, whether a loan concerns money, food or other commodities. It makes explicit that in contrast interest may be exacted from a foreigner. This reflects the distinct emphasis in Deuteronomy on staying closely connected as brothers. Indeed Moses urges the tribes who will settle East of the Jordan not to abandon their brothers in the fight West of the Jordan (Deut. 3:18-22). He seems to have had a strong sense that there would be a tendency to fragment in the promised land as indeed happened during the period of the judges.

In 2 Kings 4:1-7 we have an example of a violation of this law in the Northern kingdom. A widow cries out to Elisha because the 'person lending on a contractual basis' (*nōsheh* / נֹשֶׁה) is coming to take away her sons as slaves, the clear implication being that she cannot afford to repay either the loan or the interest charged (or both). The narrative of Nehemiah 5:1-13 shows that such a law was important in times of famine. Poor people needed an interest free loan to tie them over until the next harvest. Nehemiah puts the moneylenders under oath to rectify the situation.

Text

²⁴ ἐὰν δὲ ἀργύριον ἐκδανείσῃς τῷ ἀδελφῷ τῷ πενιχρῷ παρὰ σοί, οὐκ ἔσῃ αὐτὸν κατεπείγων, οὐκ ἐπιθήσεις αὐτῷ τόκον.	אִם־כֶּסֶף תַּלְוֶה אֶת־עַמִּי אֶת־הֶעָנִי עִמָּךְ לֹא־תִהְיֶה לוֹ כְּנֹשֶׁה לֹא־תְשִׂימוּן עָלָיו נֶשֶׁךְ׃

עָנִי, poor, needy	πενιχρός, ά, όν, poor, needy

22:24

אִם־כֶּסֶף תַּלְוֶה / ἐὰν δὲ ἀργύριον ἐκδανείσῃς

The noun 'silver' is fronted here and thus emphasised. Fronted objects frequently omit the definite object particle אֶת־. On the copulative in the LXX see the textual note to 21:4.

אֶת־עַמִּי אֶת־הֶעָנִי / τῷ ἀδελφῷ τῷ πενιχρῷ

The MT is rather strange and may presuppose אֶת־ as the preposition 'with'. However, the second אֶת־ may also be a further specification of the direct object (see *DCH s.v.* אֶת־ I. 1. COLL. 2). The LXX read: אֶת־אָחִיךָ הֶעָנִי or (given that a number of mss add σου) אֶת־אָחִיךָ הֶעָנִי.

תְשִׂימוּן / ἐπιθήσεις

The change to the 2ⁿᵈ pers. plural is curious. The LXX read the singular, cf. Sam. Pent. תשימנו (that is, 2ⁿᵈ pers. sing. with 3ʳᵈ pers. masc. suffix and *nun energicum*).

22:26-27 (Hebr. 22:25-26)

Cloak as pledge to be returned before sunset

Translation

²⁶ If you must take as pledge the cloak of your neighbour, you will return it to him before the sun goes down,

²⁷ for it is his only covering. It is his cloak for his skin. With what will he sleep? Then it will be that he will cry out to me and I will hear, for I am merciful.

Commentary

This law continues the concern of the previous law in protecting the poor from ruthless creditors. A pledge is taken when a debt is not repaid. If, however, a cloak needs to be taken as pledge (presupposing that the debtor has no other valuable possession) then it must be returned before sunset so that he does not suffer from the cold or even die of exposure. A similar law with more context is given in Deuteronomy 24:10-13.

> ¹⁰ "When you make your neighbor a loan of any sort, you shall not go into his house to collect his pledge. ¹¹ You shall stand outside, and the man to whom you make the loan shall bring the pledge out to you. ¹² And if he is a poor man, you shall not sleep in his pledge. ¹³ You shall restore to him the pledge as the sun sets, that he may sleep in his cloak and bless you. And it shall be righteousness for you before the Lord your God.

The clear assumption is that if a creditor needs to take a cloak as a pledge, the debtor must be extremely desperate. The Septuagint makes explicit what is implied in the Hebrew, namely that the debtor will have to walk around naked during the day without his cloak! Indeed, the law does specifically state that this cloak covers his 'skin'. It would seem that we are to imagine the man working during the day with only a loincloth around his waist. The motivation given at the end, that God is merciful, naturally implies that an Israelite in his dealings with his neighbour ought to reflect God's mercy (cf. Luke 6:36). Amos 2:6-8 shows that this law contained no idle warning:

> *⁶ Thus says the* LORD: *"For three transgressions of Israel, and for four, I will not revoke the punishment, because they sell the righteous for silver, and the needy for a pair of sandals — ⁷ those who trample the head of the poor into the dust of the earth and turn aside the way of the afflicted; a man and his father go in to the same girl, so that my holy name is profaned; ⁸ they lay themselves down beside every altar on garments taken in pledge, and in the house of their God they drink the wine of those who have been fined.*

Ezekiel too contrasts the righteous man who restores a pledge with the wicked man who does not (Ezek. 18:7, 12; 33:15).

This law provides a final opportunity for a poor man in debt to be given time to pay it off before he is sold into debt-slavery. In Deuteronomy 24:17 it is forbidden for a creditor to take a widow's garment as a pledge. She should not be expected to walk around during the day with nothing but a loincloth. The law also forbids creditors from taking basic tools as pledges such as a hand mill or upper millstone (Deut. 24:6, cf. Job 24:3). In addition, the creditor is barred from forcing entry into the debtor's home to retrieve a pledge (Deut. 24:10-11).

The Lord Jesus alludes to this law in the sermon on the Mount, where he is engaged in a series of deliberate exaggerations. Jesus says:

> *And if anyone would sue you and take your tunic, let him have your cloak as well.* (Matt. 5:40)

The presupposition is that a person has taken you to court to have your pledged garment (the undershirt or tunic) forfeited. Jesus, in deliberate exaggeration, suggests that one should give him one's outer cloak as well (which would literally entail walking around naked).

Text

²⁵ ἐὰν δὲ ἐνεχύρασμα ἐνεχυράσῃς τὸ ἱμάτιον τοῦ πλησίον, πρὸ δυσμῶν ἡλίου ἀποδώσεις αὐτῷ· ²⁶ ἔστιν γὰρ τοῦτο περιβόλαιον αὐτοῦ, μόνον τοῦτο τὸ ἱμάτιον ἀσχημοσύνης αὐτοῦ· ἐν τίνι κοιμηθήσεται; ἐὰν οὖν καταβοήσῃ πρός με, εἰσακούσομαι αὐτοῦ· ἐλεήμων γάρ εἰμι.	אִם־חָבֹל תַּחְבֹּל שַׂלְמַת רֵעֶךָ עַד־בֹּא הַשֶּׁמֶשׁ תְּשִׁיבֶנּוּ לוֹ׃ ⁶² כִּי הִוא כְסוּתֹה לְבַדָּהּ הִוא שִׂמְלָתוֹ לְעֹרוֹ בַּמֶּה יִשְׁכָּב וְהָיָה כִּי־יִצְעַק אֵלַי וְשָׁמַעְתִּי כִּי־חַנּוּן אָנִי׃

עוֹר, skin	ἐνεχύρασμα, ατος, τό, pledge (apart from 1 papyrus, only used in the LXX)

22:25

אִם / ἐὰν δὲ

On the question of a copulative, see the textual note to 21:4.

תַּחְבֹּל שַׂלְמַת רֵעֶךָ / ἐνεχυράσῃς τὸ ἱμάτιον τοῦ πλησίον

This appears to be the only time the verb חבל is used in the Old Testament with a definite noun phrase indicating the pledge. It is therefore unclear if we should have expected a definite object marker or whether the item taken in pledge is just a complement.

The LXX lacks the pronominal suffix, which may be presumed by the definite article. The word πλησίον is the adverb of πλησίος formed from the accusative singular ('nearby'). When used with the article as a substantive it implies the participle of the verb 'to be' and means 'the neighbour' (ὁ πλησίον ὤν / τοῦ πλησίον ὄντος).

עַד־בֹּא הַשֶּׁמֶשׁ

>The verb בא is used for the sun going down. For the rising of the sun זרח or יצא is used. Note that the preposition עד can mean 'before'.

22:26

הוּא כְסוּתֹה ... הִוא

>The *Naqdanim* have pointed for היא (twice) referring back to שַׂלְמָה and כְּסוּתוֹ referring to the neighbour. The MT spelling may be archaic.

לְבַדָּהּ

>The noun בַּד means 'part' or 'portion'. It is frequently used adverbially with לְ and a pronominal suffix in the sense 'only', i.e. 'in her (referring to the cloak) solitude'.

וְשָׁמַעְתִּי / εἰσακούσομαι αὐτοῦ

>The LXX may have read: וּשְׁמַעְתִּיו.

# 22:28 (Hebr. 22:27)

Don't declare gods or a ruler to be cursed

Translation

²⁸ You shall not declare gods (i.e. judges) to be cursed and a ruler over your people you shall not curse.

Commentary

Two parallel situations are forbidden without sanction in this law. The first is declaring 'gods' to be cursed[129] and the second to bind a curse on a ruler of the people. In both cases the sense is more than that of throwing insults (*contra* LXX), but of calling upon God / gods to curse others.

The first situation is often rendered by Bible translations as if referring to 'God' and not to 'gods'. Such a translation, however, makes little sense. Already in the introduction, in the section on 'Legal courts', I referred to the common use of the term *ᵉlōhîm* (אֱלֹהִים, 'gods') as an honorary title for 'judges' in legal contexts. When the term is coupled with a plural verb this is invariably the case. When the term is used with a singular verb, it is a plural of majesty referring to 'God'. In this verse, however, there is no finite verb showing us exactly how the term is meant to be taken. Context is therefore determinative. Given that judges are a form of ruler and that the declaration of accursedness here does not warrant a civil penalty, judges are clearly meant.[130] Declaring

---

129. Although English translations often render the verb קלל *Piel* as 'to curse', it literally refers to declaring someone to be cursed. The verb 'to curse' is ארר *Qal*.
130. See also the commentary at 21:15, 17 (cursing one's parents does incur a civil penalty). The Septuagint translates correctly 'gods' here. The Aramaic targums clearly understand the reference to be to judges. Josephus (*Ant.* 4.207;

- 156 -

God himself to be cursed would ultimately require the death penalty (Lev. 24:11-15, cf. 1 Kings 21:1-16).[131] The reason that declaring judges or rulers to be cursed is not punished by the civil courts would appear to be the fact that the principles of restitution and *lex talionis* (equitable retribution) are not easily applied to words. Defamation is not punished. God's law does not discuss the possibility of financial consequences as a result of the defamation of a person relating to his work or business. The principles of restitution and *lex talionis* could, however, be applied in such a situation. In fact, wrongful defamation of a virgin is punished with a severe financial penalty in Deuteronomy 22:13-19, given that the social implication is that such a girl would not be able to marry and therefore her parents (who receive the money) would be expected to care for her.

Ecclesiastes 10:20 reminds us that God's laws should never be treated as if they only refer to external activities. If we are told not to curse judges or rulers, then this also applies to the thoughts of our hearts. Ecclesiastes says:

> *Do not declare the king cursed, even in your thought;*
> *Do not declare the rich cursed, even in your bedroom;*
> *For a bird of the air may carry your voice,*
> *And a bird in flight may tell the matter.*

Did the apostle Paul sin against this law?

The apostle Paul would seem to have contravened the spirit of this commandment when he called the functioning high priest a 'whitewashed wall' (Acts 23:3). He more or less apologises by quoting this verse and stating that he did not realise that Ananias was high

---

contra Ap. 2.237) and Philo (*Vita Mos.* 2.205; *Quaest. in Ex.* 2.5-6; cf. *Spec.Leg.* 1.53) understand the reference to be to heathen gods! This would seem to have been a popular understanding of the text among Jews of the time.

131. This is clearly the ruling in Lev. 24, although that same passage also shows that up until that point there was no clear legal precedent, apart from the suggestive wording of the third commandment. In Lev. 24 we are told that 'boring through' God's name is punishable by death. The case in point is clearly that of a curse made against YHWH.

priest. Some expositors have suggested that Paul did not recognise the man due to poor eyesight or because he had been away overseas, but this could hardly have been the case. The high priest would have been both clear from his physical position in the courtroom and his clothing. It is possible that Paul is hinting at the fact that the high priests in Jerusalem, ever since Onias III (who reigned as high priest until 174 BC), were no longer legitimate.[132]

Text

²⁷ θεοὺς οὐ κακολογήσεις, καὶ ἄρχοντας τοῦ λαοῦ σου οὐ κακῶς ἐρεῖς.	אֱלֹהִים לֹא תְקַלֵּל וְנָשִׂיא בְעַמְּךָ לֹא תָאֹר:

---

[132]. After the Maccabean revolt the Hasmonean priests, who were not of a high-priestly lineage, had taken upon themselves the high priesthood. This illegitimate high-priestly succession was sorely felt by the Jews. The Zadokite successor Onias IV founded in protest a new temple in Leontopolis, Egypt, appealing to the fulfilment of the prophecy in Isaiah 19. Almost certainly it is also the demise of the Zadokite high-priesthood in Jerusalem that led the Qumran community to separate themselves and repudiate the Jerusalem temple. The Pharisees were also highly critical of the Hasmonean high priests. During Roman rule, high-priests were appointed from among the aristocratic priestly class by the Roman governors or by others to whom the Romans gave the rights of appointment.

Words for Cursing

אלה *Qal* to utter a (self-imprecating) conditional curse, *Hiph.* to adjure (make to utter a conditional curse) – *a judicial term referring to the curse portion of an oath*

Related Noun:

אָלָה, curse (the words praying for God to give potential punishment); 2. realised curse, a) the punishments, b) the actual punishment applied to a particular person

To lay a curse on someone is expressed in several ways, e.g.: נָשָׂא אָלָה בְּ / נָתַן אָלָה עַל / הֵבִיא אָלָה עַל

To make someone a cursed person (2b): נָתַן לְאָלָה / הָיָה לְאָלָה

ארר *Qal* to bind with a curse (i.e. to curse someone/something else), *Piel* to make to be cursed (e.g. a field, water)

Related Noun:

מְאֵרָה, curse (i.e. a curse that has been spoken by one person against another person or thing)

קלל *Qal* to be small, insignificant, *Piel* to declare to be insignificant (i.e. to make a person to be small or contemptible by means of verbal insult). *This verb is also sometimes used of cursing, which is of course a particularly strong kind of insult.*

Related Noun:

קְלָלָה, curse-formula, 2. the actual curse

קבב *Qal* to utter a curse against someone/something.

22:29-31 (Hebr. 22:28-30)

Dedications to God: first-fruits, first-born animals, Israelites

Translation

²⁹ You shall not delay your harvest or your juice. The first-born of your sons you shall give to me.

³⁰ Thus you shall do for your cattle and for your flock, it will remain seven days with its mother, on the eighth day you will give it to me.

³¹ But you will be holy men to me and you shall not eat torn flesh-in-the-field. You shall throw it to the dog.

Commentary

The laws given here are brief and provide no details. They concern those things that belong to God, namely first-fruits, first-born animals and even the Israelites themselves, who are specifically said to be 'holy'. Verse 31 (v.30 of the Hebrew) concerning the Israelites is directly connected to the preceding verses by what is known in Hebrew grammar as a circumstantial clause (the order conjunction – subject – verb instead of conjunction – verb – subject). The term 'holy' refers to what belongs to God. There is therefore a real sense in which the Israelites, just as first-fruits and first-born animals are God's property.

First-fruits: An ancient custom

First-fruits and first-born are to be paid to God and there is to be no delay. The concern is to remind the people to be prompt and willing in their obedience. The law implies that the custom of giving first-fruits to God was well-known and that the rituals and procedures did not need to be specified. In fact, directly after the Exodus the implications of the tenth plague for the giving of first-born were spelled out to the people (Exod. 13:11-16[133]). The story of Abraham's potential sacrifice of Isaac shows that the principle goes right back to the patriarchs (Gen. 22) and even the beginning of mankind, given that Abel too is said to have brought the first-fruits of his flock to the Lord (Gen. 4:4).

First-fruits of the harvest

Although the term 'first-fruits' is not specifically mentioned here, the context makes it clear that this is what is meant. Literally the law states: "You shall not delay your harvest or your juice".[134] The requirement for paying first-fruits from the land is made specific in Exodus 23:19 (= 34:26; see also Num. 15:18-21 and compare 2Kgs 4:42). In Numbers 18:12-18 we are told that these first-fruits, which are dedicated to YHWH, may be consumed by the priests in God's temple (cf. Deut. 18:4). The laws make it clear that a tribute of first-fruits was to be made from harvested grain, oil and wine ('juices') and also (after entry into the promised land) from the fleece of the first-shearing of sheep (Deut. 18:4). A sheaf from the first-fruits was to be brought to the temple on the first Sunday after the beginning of the harvest. Exactly seven weeks later, on the day of Pentecost, the first-fruit offerings were to be brought. The prescribed first-fruit offerings were not large. For grain this amounted to one sheaf immediately after the beginning of the harvest and two baked bread-loaves at Pentecost (as well as the stipulated sacrifices).[135] The point was that every land-holder had to acknowledge that his harvest and increase came from the

---

133. This legal text gives the law as it applied in the promised land. Given that it speaks of the redemption of first-born sons, the law clarifies to the reader (presumed to be in the promised land) what the law means for him now. The transition from first-born sons dedicated to God to first-born sons being redeemed only actually occurred at Mt. Sinai (see below).
134. The nouns used here are actually very rare in these senses in Hebrew. The text refers more literally to "your fullness and your tears". For discussion and the tradition of interpretation see other commentaries. Later Hebrew and Aramaic take the terms as they are generally given in translations and interpreted here.
135. For more information see Anderson[5].

Lord. He was, after all, working God's land, for which reason land in Israel could not be sold or given away.

First-fruits of living beings

First-born male domesticated animals and humans were to be dedicated to Yhwh as well (cf. Exod. 34:19-20). Before the sin with the golden calf, there is every indication that first-born males were dedicated as priests (cf. 1 Sam. 1:11). It was only as a result of that sin and the aftermath, when only the Levites stood by Moses for Yhwh, that he agreed to take the Levites as his personnel (Exod. 32).[136] Numbers three describes how the first-born sons of the people were substituted for the Levites. Those who did not have a Levite to substitute for them had to pay a redemption price of five temple shekels.

First-born animals or humans were only acceptable to God after they had been with their mother for seven days. For this reason circumcision occurred on the eighth day and animals had to be given to God on the eighth day (Gen. 17:12; Exod. 22:19). While Israel was encamped at Mt. Sinai, this was certainly possible, although the law of Leviticus 22:27 already modifies this provision by stating that the animal is acceptable for sacrifice from the eighth day onward. Numbers 18:11-19 explains further that all first-fruits, whether of grain, wine, oil or animal were to be available for consumption in the sanctuary by the priests. It also explains that while first-born males from clean animals were to be sacrificed, first-born males from unclean animals were to be redeemed, as were the first-born sons. Exodus 34:20 had already stipulated that the first-born of donkeys had to be either redeemed with a lamb or have their neck broken.[137] In Deuteronomy 15:19-22 the law was further modified, taking account of the new situation in the promised land with one central sanctuary, which was no longer so

---

136. See the appendix on the effect of the sin of the golden calf.
137. An unclean animal could not be sacrificed, but the act of breaking its neck made it a gift to the Lord (cf. David's libation of water, 2 Sam. 23:15-16). Numbers 18:15-16 gives the option of redeeming the first-born of unclean animals (one month after birth) for 5 silver shekels, presumably the equivalent value of a lamb. Interestingly, this is the same amount required to redeem a first-born son (Num. 3:47).

close-by to everybody. First-born animals now had to be brought to the sanctuary at one of the feasts within a year of their birth, where they might be eaten by the worshippers. Deuteronomy explains, however, that if there is a defect this dedication is cancelled and the animal may be eaten outside the sanctuary. First-born male animals were never to be worked or sheared. In the case of first-born humans dedicated to God, we see Samuel being brought to the temple only after the period of weaning (1 Sam. 1:22).

Jesus Christ, being the first-born son of Joseph and Mary, had to be redeemed in the temple (cf. Luke 2:23). Jesus himself, although of the tribe of Judah, later became high-priest according to the order of Melchizedek, following the prophecy of Psalm 110 (discussed *in extenso* in the letter to the Hebrews). His high-priesthood, however, applies not to the earthly, but to the heavenly sanctuary. Jesus is also considered to be the first-born Son of God himself (Col. 1:15) as well as the first-born from the dead (Col. 1:18; Rev. 1:5). The letter to the Hebrews characterises believers in Jesus Christ as 'first-born', that is, priests serving God before the heavenly sanctuary in which Jesus Christ ministers (Hebr. 12:22-24).

The holiness of the Israelites

The final verse of this law specifically ties the command not to eat the meat of an animal torn by beasts to the holiness of the Israelites. In other words, we are once again dealing with a commandment related to ritual purity. In Exodus 19:6 God had already called the Israelites "a kingdom of priests and a holy nation". 'Holiness' in this sense was the ritual status given to priests as property of God.[138] Although at this point in Israel's history it was still the case that first-born sons were to be dedicated to God as priests (see above), nevertheless in a limited sense the status of holiness was made to apply to every single Israelite, male and female. The command not to eat the flesh of a torn field-animal is a case in point. In fact, it was specifically forbidden for priests and – as a holy nation – all Israelites to eat any animal that had not been appropriately slaughtered (cf. Lev. 7:24; 17:15-16; Ezek. 4:14; 44:31). Eating such meat made one ritually unclean and

---

138. See Anderson[4], § 1.2.

therefore unfit to appear before God.[139] It required ritual purification by washing one's clothes, bathing in 'living' water and waiting until evening before he was ritually clean again.[140] God expected all uncleanness, whether caused by sin or non-avoidable duties or acts, to be purified. Israel was his people by covenant and their holy status had to be maintained.

It is interesting that, although the Book of the Covenant mentions various ritual regulations, it does not discuss the concept of uncleanness or the matter of purification rituals. Nevertheless, the fact that this law is motivated by the command to be (ritually) 'holy', presupposes that the Israelites were already familiar with the concepts of ritual purity.

The dog rewarded

The meat of an animal torn in the field may be thrown "to the dog". The presumption appears to be that such an animal would have been attacked in the field where the shepherd with his dog was tending the flock. The attacked animal was not completely devoured, perhaps because the dog prevented that. In any case, the dog may profit from the misadventure.[141] The clear implication is that the meat is unfit for human consumption. At first glance this seems to contradict the law of Deuteronomy 14:21.

> *You shall not eat anything that has died naturally. You may give it to the sojourner who is within your towns, that he may eat it, or you may sell it to a foreigner. For you are a people holy to the* LORD *your God.*

Here the same ritual motivation of being 'holy' to God is applied to animals that have 'died naturally'. Actually the phrase "anything that

---

139. It should be noted that while the eating of unclean animals was forbidden and sinful, such eating did not make a person ritually unclean. Merely touching the carcass of an unclean animal would, however, make one unclean. In Exod. 22:31 it is the eating (not the touching) of the carcass of an animal (clean or unclean) that had not been appropriately slaughtered (i.e. having its blood drained) that makes one ritually unclean and in need of purification.
140. See Anderson[4], § 1.4a.
141. Dogs were already used by the Israelites in Egypt (cf. Exod. 11:10). For watchdogs over the flock in Israel cf. Isa. 56:10-11; Job 30:1.

has died naturally" refers literally to a 'carcass' (*nᵉvēlah* / נְבֵלָה). Such a carcass, however, is not thrown to dogs, but given as meat to a resident alien or sold to a foreigner.[142] It is clear, however, that animals that had already been torn by a wild beast were to be considered a separate category. Already in Leviticus 17:15 they are listed separately, next to carcasses. What this means is that, although neither carcasses nor animals torn by beasts are to be eaten by Israelites, carcasses may be eaten by people in Israel who are not Yhwh worshippers. Animals torn by beasts may be disposed of in other ways, for example as food for the dog (cf. Lev. 7:24 which simply stipulates 'other use' for the fat of such an animal).

Text

²⁸ ἀπαρχὰς ἅλωνος καὶ ληνοῦ σου οὐ καθυστερήσεις· τὰ πρωτότοκα τῶν υἱῶν σου δώσεις ἐμοί. ²⁹ οὕτως ποιήσεις τὸν μόσχον σου καὶ τὸ πρόβατόν σου καὶ τὸ ὑποζύγιόν σου· ἑπτὰ ἡμέρας ἔσται ὑπὸ τὴν μητέρα, τῇ δὲ ἡμέρᾳ τῇ ὀγδόῃ ἀποδώσεις μοι αὐτό. ³⁰ καὶ ἄνδρες ἅγιοι ἔσεσθέ μοι. καὶ κρέας θηριάλωτον οὐκ ἔδεσθε, τῷ κυνὶ ἀπορρίψατε αὐτό.	מְלֵאָתְךָ וְדִמְעֲךָ לֹא תְאַחֵר בְּכוֹר בָּנֶיךָ תִּתֶּן־לִי: ²⁹ כֵּן־תַּעֲשֶׂה לְשֹׁרְךָ לְצֹאנֶךָ שִׁבְעַת יָמִים יִהְיֶה עִם־אִמּוֹ בַּיּוֹם הַשְּׁמִינִי תִּתְּנוֹ־לִי: ³⁰ וְאַנְשֵׁי־קֹדֶשׁ תִּהְיוּן לִי וּבָשָׂר בַּשָּׂדֶה טְרֵפָה לֹא תֹאכֵלוּ לַכֶּלֶב תַּשְׁלִכוּן אֹתוֹ:
דֶּמַע, juice אחר, *Piel* to delay, linger	καθυστερέω, to come (too) late

---

142. The resident alien / sojourner (i.e. a refugee with limited rights in the society) may benefit without charge as charity. The foreign trader must buy the meat. Deuteronomy is obviously thinking of a resident alien who is not concerned with the laws of purity and thus a person who is not a worshipper of Yhwh.

22:28

מְלֵאָתְךָ וְדִמְעֲךָ / ἀπαρχὰς ἅλωνος καὶ ληνοῦ σου

The translation makes the vagueness of the Hebrew more specific. Note the omission of אֶת-, which is common when the direct object precedes the verb. The same holds true for the ensuing בְּכוֹר בָּנֶיךָ.

22:29

καὶ τὸ ὑποζύγιόν σου

The addition makes little sense if referring to donkeys. Unclean first-born were to have their necks broken or be redeemed.

בַּיּוֹם הַשְּׁמִינִי / τῇ δὲ ἡμέρᾳ τῇ ὀγδόῃ

The LXX and Sam. Pent. both read the extra *waw*.

22:30

וְאַנְשֵׁי־קֹדֶשׁ

The order conjunction – subject – verb connects this verse to the preceding by what is usually called a circumstantial clause.

וּבָשָׂר בַּשָּׂדֶה טְרֵפָה / κρέας θηριάλωτον

The prepositional phrase coming between the noun and its adjective is odd. It seems to serve little purpose, restricting the torn flesh which may not be eaten to that found in one's field. The scenario is, of course, that in which a wild animal has entered a farmer's field and killed one of his domestic animals. Such an animal may not be eaten.

תֹאכֵלוּ / ἔδεσθε

The LXX in this portion of the translation uses the Attic future of ἐσθίω (Jewish-Greek for the Hellenistic τρώγω) instead of the Hellenistic φάγομαι, cf. 23:11, 14, see Anderson[10], 'Eating in Greek' following *Animal Story* 18.

תַּשְׁלִכוּן / ἀπορρίψατε

The verb שׁלך is only found in the *Hiphil / Hophal*, but is tentatively explained as the causative of הלך, the *sha-* being a causative element. The LXX probably did not read: הַשְׁלִכוּן (imperative), but typically translates the Hebrew imperfect of commands with an imperative.

23:1-3

Don't give false evidence, follow the majority in evil or be partial in a dispute

Translation

¹ You shall not speak[143] a vain report. Don't set your hand with a wicked person to be a false witness[144]

² You shall not follow the many for wickedness and you shall not testify in a lawsuit[145] to turn aside after the many to divert judgment

³ and the poor you shall not honour in his lawsuit.

Commentary

These three verses belong together and as such should probably be understood as having primary reference to a courtroom setting. Verse one can be taken to refer to the influence which an individual may have over the many, while verse two reckons with the influence that the many may have over an individual.

It is, at first sight, unclear whether verse one is referring to the *spreading* or to the *acceptance* of a vain report. The Hebrew verb (*nāsā'* / נשׂא) could mean either 'to spread' (a report) or, as the Septuagint understands it, 'to receive' (a report). In the latter sense, the law would be speaking to a judge, but this does not accord so

---

143. Lit. 'lift up', i.e. upon your lips.
144. Lit. 'witness of violence', the standard idiom for what we call a 'false witness'.
145. Lit. 'reply upon a lawsuit', which refers to the reply of the opposition in a legal case.

well with the context of these verses, which refer to bearing false witness. Houtman points to Exodus 20:7 ("You shall not lift up the name of YHWH your God in vain") and argues that "lifting up a vain report" should in fact refer to speaking a vain report. That is to say, one lifts up a report upon one's lips. The text is therefore not explicitly forbidding rumour-mongering (as Lev. 19:16 in fact does). The two clauses of verse one should therefore be viewed as parallel to each other. When one speaks a vain/false report, he is by that fact acting as a false witness.[146]

A concrete example of such a false report taken to court can be found in Deuteronomy 22:13-19 where a girl is wrongly accused, after marriage, of not having been a virgin. An historical example can be found in 1 Kings 21 (Naboth).

As suggested above, verse two speaks of the influence of the many over an individual. Once again the two clauses are parallel to each other. Even if most people pervert justice by twisting the facts, one must dare to stand firm upon the truth, trusting in the God of truth.[147]

A final way of perverting justice is mentioned in verse three, namely, unjustly wreaking vengeance on the wealthy by showing partiality to the poor in his dispute. A similar warning is given in Leviticus 19:15.[148]

It is noteworthy that these warnings are given without mention of penal sanctions and are included in this non-penal section of the law-code. In fact, penal sanctions were introduced for bearing false witness only some 40 years later, when Moses promulgated the law-code of Deuteronomy (see Deut. 19:15-21). At this time, the *lex talionis*

---

146. The phrase literally means "witness of violence" (עֵד חָמָס) and is the regular way of expressing a false witness, see Deut. 19:16 (see the parallel in v.18 עֵד שֶׁקֶר) and Ps. 35:11.

147. The LXX adds 'justice' at the end of the verse. The Hebrew leaves 'to pervert' without an object. Sarna takes רַבִּים to refer to 'mighty men' in an attempt to connect this verse, by means of contrast, to the poor of v.3. The attempt remains unconvincing.

148. Some scholars have proposed an emendation (for details see the textual commentary), which would make the text speak of the 'great' man instead of the 'poor' man. The LXX, however, does read 'poor' and the same point is made in Lev. 19:15. There is therefore no need to emend the text.

(see the introduction) was applied not only to victims who had been physically maimed, but also to false witnesses, who by their testimony were condemning others to wrongful punishment.

Text

23 Οὐ παραδέξῃ ἀκοὴν ματαίαν· οὐ συγκαταθήσῃ μετὰ τοῦ ἀδίκου γενέσθαι μάρτυς ἄδικος. ² οὐκ ἔσῃ μετὰ πλειόνων ἐπὶ κακίᾳ· οὐ προστεθήσῃ μετὰ πλήθους ἐκκλῖναι μετὰ πλειόνων ὥστε ἐκκλῖναι κρίσιν. ³ καὶ πένητα οὐκ ἐλεήσεις ἐν κρίσει.	לֹא תִשָּׂא שֵׁמַע שָׁוְא אַל־תָּשֶׁת יָדְךָ עִם־רָשָׁע לִהְיֹת עֵד חָמָס: ² לֹא־תִהְיֶה אַחֲרֵי־רַבִּים לְרָעֹת וְלֹא־תַעֲנֶה עַל־רִב לִנְטֹת אַחֲרֵי רַבִּים לְהַטֹּת: ³ וְדָל לֹא תֶהְדַּר בְּרִיבוֹ:

דַּל, low, poor, helpless (cf. דלל, 'to become tiny')	הדר, *Qal* to honour

23:1

לֹא תִשָּׂא שֵׁמַע שָׁוְא / Οὐ παραδέξῃ ἀκοὴν ματαίαν

See the main commentary on the question of the interpretation of נשא here.

אַל־תָּשֶׁת יָדְךָ עִם־רָשָׁע

The verb שׁית with יָד (often with pronominal suffix) is an idiom which does not use אֶת־. In fact, the omission of אֶת־ is not uncommon when the direct object is a body-part, cf. Joüon/Muraoka §125ia. Gen. 48:14, 17 provides an interesting illustration:

וַיִּשְׁלַח יִשְׂרָאֵל אֶת־יְמִינוֹ וַיָּשֶׁת עַל־רֹאשׁ אֶפְרַיִם

וַיַּרְא יוֹסֵף כִּי־יָשִׁית אָבִיו יַד־יְמִינוֹ עַל־רֹאשׁ אֶפְרַיִם

This is the only place where 'laying/setting a hand' is coupled with the preposition עִם. It seems to imply 'joining the hand with'.

23:2

וְלֹא־תַעֲנֶה עַל־רִב / οὐ προστεθήσῃ μετὰ πλήθους
The LXX appears to have read: לֹא־תֵּאָסֵף עַל־רִב.

לִנְטֹת אַחֲרֵי רַבִּים
The verb נטה is used in an inwardly-transitive sense here 'to turn aside' (lit. 'to stretch oneself out').

לְהַטֹּת / ὥστε ἐκκλῖναι κρίσιν
See v.6. It would seem that we need to understand מִשְׁפָּט as object, cf. LXX.

23:3

וְדָל לֹא תֶהְדַּר / καὶ πένητα οὐκ ἐλεήσεις
On the basis of Lev. 19:15 לֹא־תִשָּׂא פְנֵי־דָל וְלֹא תֶהְדַּר פְּנֵי גָדוֹל, some interpreters suggest emending וְדָל to גָּדֹל. See the main commentary for a refutation of this suggestion. The LXX may or may not suggest the reading: תְּרַחֵם for תֶהְדַּר. Note that the clause is circumstantial.

23:4-5

Help your enemy's animal in trouble

Translation

⁴ When you encounter a head of cattle or donkey of your enemy wandering aimlessly, you shall certainly return it to him.

⁵ When you see the donkey of someone who hates you lying down under its load, you will cease from leaving it to him, you will surely help him raise it back up.[149]

Commentary

Two practical examples of loving one's enemy are now provided (cf. Matt. 5:43-44 and also Prov. 24:17-18). The law thus stimulates caring for the property of others, even when they may be personal enemies. Durham[150] states appropriately:

> "The point at issue in these two verses is not so much a humane attitude toward a lost or improperly laden animal as it is a refusal to take advantage of another's misfortunes because he happens to be an enemy. The loose animal is usually enjoying himself, and the animal that lies down under a poorly arranged load is protecting himself. The one at risk here is the owner, who may lose a valuable animal altogether or have to unload and reload an animal in an insecure spot and without help".

The situation envisaged here is quite different from the sort of enemy loathed in the psalms, who is clearly an enemy of God himself (cf. Ps. 139:19-22). The law deliberately speaks both of 'your enemy' and

---

149. The text at the end of v.5 is difficult, although the general gist is not in doubt (cf. the parallel in Deut. 22:4). See the textual commentary for details.
150. Durham, vol.3, 331.

'the person who hates you', implying that the principle holds both in the situation that one is at enmity with another person and when another person is at enmity with oneself. The feelings do not have to be reciprocal. It is important to note that the verb 'to hate' in Hebrew (*sānā'* / שׂנא) can denote anything from absolute hatred to just not wanting anything to do with someone.

Moses gives a more detailed variation on these laws in Deuteronomy 22:1-4. There, however, the emphasis is on how the property is to be cared for, whatever animal – or even clothing – is lost and found by someone else. In Exodus the emphasis is on the fact that such care *also* applies to one's personal enemy.

Text

⁴ Ἐὰν δὲ συναντήσῃς τῷ βοΐ τοῦ ἐχθροῦ σου ἢ τῷ ὑποζυγίῳ αὐτοῦ πλανωμένοις, ἀποστρέψας ἀποδώσεις αὐτῷ. ⁵ Ἐὰν δὲ ἴδῃς τὸ ὑποζύγιον τοῦ ἐχθροῦ σου πεπτωκὸς ὑπὸ τὸν γόμον αὐτοῦ, οὐ παρελεύσῃ αὐτό, ἀλλὰ συνεγερεῖς αὐτὸ μετ' αὐτοῦ.	כִּי תִפְגַּע שׁוֹר אֹיִבְךָ אוֹ חֲמֹרוֹ תֹּעֶה הָשֵׁב תְּשִׁיבֶנּוּ לוֹ: ⁵ כִּי־תִרְאֶה חֲמוֹר שֹׂנַאֲךָ רֹבֵץ תַּחַת מַשָּׂאוֹ וְחָדַלְתָּ מֵעֲזֹב לוֹ עָזֹב תַּעֲזֹב עִמּוֹ:

פגע, *Qal* to encounter תעה, *Qal* to wander about, err רבץ, *Qal* to lie down, rest	עזב, *Qal* to leave behind, forsake עור, *Qal* to be awake; *Hiph.* to rouse, to excite / put into motion γόμος, ὁ, freight, load

23:4-5

כִּי / Ἐὰν δὲ

On the question of a copulative, see the textual note to 21:4.

תִפְגַּע שׁוֹר אֹיִבְךָ אוֹ חֲמֹרוֹ ... תִרְאֶה חֲמוֹר שֹׂנַאֲךָ

We might have expected the use of definite object markers. It may be that the animals are not individuated here because the reference is not to specific beasts. In any case, when the definite object marker is not used, the direct object usually follows directly upon the verb, as here. In English, therefore, we may translate 'a head of cattle of your enemy', despite the Hebrew literally speaking of 'the head of cattle of your enemy'. Note the Hebrew idiom: 'the head of cattle of your enemy or his donkey'. In Hebrew, given the constraints of the construct relationship, one cannot say: 'The head of cattle or donkey of your enemy'.

שֹׂנַאֲךָ

We should note that Hebrew distinguishes the *Qal* from the *Piel* participle of שׂנא. The *Qal* often indicates a concrete person, while the *Piel* is used in reference to that person or persons who naturally or professionally are given to hating.[151] It is important to note that the verb can denote anything from absolute hatred to just not wanting anything to do with someone. When used of a husband or wife, it can merely indicate the absence of love.[152]

תְּשִׁיבֶנּוּ / ἀποδώσεις

The LXX omits the pronominal suffix.

כִּי־תִרְאֶה : לוֹ / αὐτῷ. ⁵ Ἐὰν δὲ ἴδῃς

The LXX may have read two *waws* succeeding each other, but see the textual note to 21:4.

וְחָדַלְתָּ מֵעֲזֹב לוֹ עָזֹב תַּעֲזֹב עִמּוֹ / οὐ παρελεύσῃ αὐτό, ἀλλὰ συνεγερεῖς αὐτὸ μετ' αὐτοῦ

These phrases are difficult. To begin with what is simple, the verb חדל often takes מן + the infinitive construct in the sense 'to cease from doing *something*'. This would give us: 'And you will cease from forsaking ...'. However the verb עזב takes an accusative. It is not one of the small number of Hebrew verbs which uses ל to indicate the accusative. If we can presuppose the direct object from the context, then the preposition ל would indicate leaving something to someone. This would give us: 'And you will cease from leaving (it) to him'. The use of the same verb in the next phrase is so puzzling that many

---

151. Jenni[2], *Piel*, 224.
152. Jenni[3].

interpreters have supposed that there must be a homonym עזב with a different meaning. This has been seriously questioned, however, and not without cause. Would the author really use two homonyms with virtually opposite meanings in such close proximity to each other? Ought we not rather to suppose that some corruption has entered the textual tradition? The LXX would suggest something like וְעוֹר תְּעִירָהוּ עִמּוֹ or alternately וְהַעֲיר(וֹ)תוֹ. Then we would render: 'You will (surely) help him raise it back up' (cf. Deut. 22:4 הָקֵם תָּקִים עִמּוֹ). If one desires to stay closer to the consonants of the MT, it is possible to read: עָזֹר תַּעֲזֹר עִמּוֹ ('you will surely render help with him'), however the preposition עִם is not idiomatic with this verb and we should then have expected לְ. The NKJV reads וְחָדַלְתָּ as a jussive, but this would require וְיֶחְדַּלְתָּ.

23:6-9

Don't pervert justice, take a bribe or oppress a sojourner

Translation

⁶ You shall not pervert the justice of your poor man in his lawsuit.

⁷ You will keep yourself far from a lying word. You shall kill neither an innocent nor a righteous person, for I will not justify a wicked person.

⁸ And you shall not take a gift, for a gift blinds the eyes of those able to see and twists the words of righteous persons.

⁹ And you shall not oppress a sojourner, since you know the soul of a sojourner for you were sojourners in the land of Egypt.

Commentary

These four verses form a series of circumstantial clauses in Hebrew, which show that they are to be taken together as one unit. While 23:1-3 warned against perverting justice from the point of view of a witness, the following law is addressed to the elders in the gate or judges. The elders / judges are addressed as individuals in the singular. They are to ensure that justice is fair and righteous. The poor are described as 'your poor', given that they are entirely in the hands of the judges and have no other recourse or backup. The pronoun thus serves to emphasise the responsibility of the judges to the poor. They are not to wrongly condemn an innocent person to death (cf. the case of Naboth in 1 Kings 21).

The third clause of verse seven can be understood in various ways. In the Massoretic text it reads: "for I will not justify a wicked person". If the 'wicked' is understood as a wicked judge, then God is promising to punish judges who contravene this law. As already noted above (see the introduction), judges render justice in the name of God and therefore receive the honorary title of 'gods'. God himself, however, will call them to account for their conduct (cf. Psalm 82).

Another possibility is that the 'wicked' refers to a guilty person who has been wrongly declared innocent by the judges. In this case, the law is stating that God, who would be expected to ratify the decisions of his judges (the 'gods'), will in such a case *not* do so.

It is, however, also possible – though perhaps less probable – to understand the words "I will not justify a wicked person" as a reference to overly zealous judges who are concerned that a possibly guilty party may escape punishment. For this reason, they may knowingly admit false evidence to secure a conviction of someone whom they are convinced is guilty. God would then be saying that judges ought not to be scared of not punishing possibly guilty people due to insufficient evidence. He himself will not justify the wicked.

Finally, the Septuagint has preserved a quite different reading which has led a number of interpreters to suggest that the Massoretic text has been corrupted. It reads: "and you will not justify the ungodly for the sake of gifts". This gives the second and third clauses of the verse an appropriate balance between not wrongly condemning the innocent or justifying the ungodly.[153] It may well be the correct reading.

The judges are expressly forbidden to receive 'gifts', a problem that seems to have been quite prevalent (cf. Deut. 27:25; 1 Sam. 8:3; Isa. 1:23; 5:23; 33:15; Ezek. 22:12; Amos 5:12; Mic. 7:3; Ps. 15:5; 26:10).[154] God himself is elsewhere described as a judge who takes no gifts (Deut. 10:17; 2 Chron. 19:7).

---

153. See the textual commentary for details.
154. The Hebrew word used denotes a 'gift' (שׁחד), which, depending on the context, may be interpreted as a 'bribe'.

The law here adds that judges also need to ensure that the justice due to a sojourner (i.e. a 'refugee', see the explanation at 22:21) is not perverted (cf. Deut. 1:16; 24:17; 27:19; Mal. 3:5). They are encouraged to remember that Israel was once in the precarious position of being refugees in Egypt.

A similar law is given in Deuteronomy 16:19 which adds a warning against partiality:

> *You shall not pervert justice. You shall not show partiality, and you shall not accept a bribe, for a bribe blinds the eyes of the wise and subverts the cause of the righteous.*

Text

⁶ Οὐ διαστρέψεις κρίμα πένητος ἐν κρίσει αὐτοῦ. ⁷ ἀπὸ παντὸς ῥήματος ἀδίκου ἀποστήσῃ· ἀθῷον καὶ δίκαιον οὐκ ἀποκτενεῖς, καὶ οὐ δικαιώσεις τὸν ἀσεβῆ ἕνεκεν δώρων. ⁸ καὶ δῶρα οὐ λήμψῃ· τὰ γὰρ δῶρα ἐκτυφλοῖ ὀφθαλμοὺς βλεπόντων καὶ λυμαίνεται ῥήματα δίκαια. ⁹ καὶ προσήλυτον οὐ θλίψετε· ὑμεῖς γὰρ οἴδατε τὴν ψυχὴν τοῦ προσηλύτου· αὐτοὶ γὰρ προσήλυτοι ἦτε ἐν γῇ Αἰγύπτῳ.	⁷ לֹא תַטֶּה מִשְׁפַּט אֶבְיֹנְךָ בְּרִיבוֹ: מִדְּבַר־שֶׁקֶר תִּרְחָק וְנָקִי וְצַדִּיק אַל־תַּהֲרֹג כִּי לֹא־אַצְדִּיק רָשָׁע: ⁸ וְשֹׁחַד לֹא תִקָּח כִּי הַשֹּׁחַד יְעַוֵּר פִּקְחִים וִיסַלֵּף דִּבְרֵי צַדִּיקִים: ⁹ וְגֵר לֹא תִלְחָץ וְאַתֶּם יְדַעְתֶּם אֶת־נֶפֶשׁ הַגֵּר כִּי־גֵרִים הֱיִיתֶם בְּאֶרֶץ מִצְרָיִם:
עור, *Piel* to make to be blind פִּקֵּחַ, able to see (*adj.*, cf. פקח 'to open [the eyes])	סלף, *Piel* to twist, misrepresent

23:6

לֹא תַטֶּה מִשְׁפַּט

This use of נטה again stems from the inwardly-transitive *Qal* 'to turn aside' (i.e. 'to stretch oneself out'). In the *Hiphil* we therefore get 'to cause oneself to stretch (justice) out', that is, 'to pervert justice'. For a possible explanation of the omission of אֶת־ see the note to 23:4.

אֶבְיֹנְךָ / πένητος

The LXX omits the pronominal suffix. Although the suffix is a little odd, it serves to emphasis the corporate responsibility for the poor among the brotherhood.

23:7

מִדְּבַר־שֶׁקֶר / ἀπὸ παντὸς ῥήματος ἀδίκου

The LXX presupposes: מִכָּל־דְּבַר־שֶׁקֶר.

ἀποστήσῃ

Curiously, the future middle, which in regular Greek is always transitive, is used here in an intransitive sense. We should have expected ἀποστηθήσῃ.

וְנָקִי וְצַדִּיק / ἀθῷον καὶ δίκαιον

The LXX omits the first *waw* and thus suggests that both adjectives belong to the same category of person. The Hebrew suggests two slightly distinct categories. Presumably an innocent person does not necessarily have to be righteous.

כִּי לֹא־אַצְדִּיק רָשָׁע / καὶ οὐ δικαιώσεις τὸν ἀσεβῆ ἕνεκεν δώρων

The LXX appears to have read: וְלֹא־תַצְדִּיק הָרָשָׁע עַל־שֹׁחַד which may suggest haplography in the MT or alternately dittography in the text used by the LXX translator. Note that the noun שֹׁחַד is used both as a singular and as a collective. The use of the *Hiphil* of צדק (and not *Piel*) shows that a judicial pronouncement is meant, see Jenni[2], 43-45. If MT is correct, the point may be that God is expected to ratify the decisions of the 'gods' (i.e. the human judges). On the Jewish use of δικαιόω, see Anderson[10], 'A note on δικαιόω' following *Animal Story* 15.

23:8

יְעַוֵּר פִּקְחִים / ἐκτυφλοῖ ὀφθαλμοὺς βλεπόντων

The LXX together with the Sam. Pent. and a ms from Qumran read יְעַוֵּר עֵינֵי פִקְחִים, cf. Deut. 16:19. This strongly indicates haplography on the part of the MT.

דִּבְרֵי צַדִּיקִים / ῥήματα δίκαια

The LXX appears to have read: דְּבָרִים צַדִּיקִים.

23:10-11

Six years of sowing, one year of rest

Translation

¹⁰ Six years you may sow your land and harvest its increase,

¹¹ but in the seventh you will let it drop and leave it fallow and the poor of your people may eat and the domestic animals[155] may eat the leftovers. Thus you shall do for your vineyard and your olive plantation.

Commentary

The law of the sabbath year is further explained in Leviticus 25:1-7, 18-22. The land was not to be sown, but to lie fallow. Grapes, olives and other fruit were not to be harvested. The law is given as an extension to the principle of the seventh day set apart as a sabbath dedicated to God. There is no mention of any benefit in terms of soil rejuvenation. By observing the seventh year as a sabbath year, the Israelites were to acknowledge that God was the owner of the land. In a sense that no other country could claim, the land of Israel was considered to be temple land. For this reason land could not be bought or sold. It was made available by God to his people for farming.[156]

It should be noted that this sabbath year did not apply to the flocks and herds, which could continue to be used for milk, meat, leather and sacrifice. The law allows for the poor to eat from whatever would grow on the land during the sabbath year, giving the leftovers to the flocks and herds which would be allowed to graze the fields and thus fertilise them with their manure. The fact that the poor were given

---

155. Lit. "the living thing / animal of the field".
156. See further Anderson⁶, §§ 1-2.

first access to what grew in the seventh year has not infrequently led expositors to suggest that the law forms part of the social regulations for care of the poor in Israel, a contention which is, however, rather far-fetched. Allowing the poor to eat from the land once every seven years would hardly alleviate poverty. What it does do, is compensate the poor for the fact that in a sabbath year no day-labourers would be employed for harvesting. We are not told how the harvest feasts of Pentecost and Booths were to be celebrated in the sabbath year. Deuteronomy 31:10 makes it plain that they were, however, still to be observed. Presumably the feasting was to be provided from the storehouses. God had promised that if they observed the sabbath year, the harvest of the sixth year would be extra abundant (cf. Lev. 25:18-22) It is also obvious that there would be no income for the sanctuary in the form of tithes in the sabbath year, except by way of the additions to flocks and herds.

Fallow land in ancient farming

It has been claimed that the idea of the whole nation letting all their fields lie fallow during the same year is surely highly impracticable. Hopkins, however, has shown that in ancient times it was quite common to let half one's land lie fallow and sow the other half on an annual basis, alternating year by year. Given this practice, farmers would actually only lose half their yield during the sabbath year. In fact, they might choose to double their yield the year before by sowing both halves of the land in the sixth year. Hopkins illustrates such a possibility using the following table, where the two rows represent the two halves of a farmer's fields and the numbered columns represent years[157]:

1st half	C	F	C	F	C	C	S	F	C	F	C	F	C	S
2nd half	F	C	F	C	F	C	S	C	F	C	F	C	C	S
Year	1	2	3	4	5	6	7	1	2	3	4	5	6	7

C = crop; F = fallow; S = sabbatical year

---

157. Hopkins, 201. The whole discussion of fallowing and land-use intensity in the ancient highlands of Canaan can be found on pages 192-202.

The real point is that leaving the land fallow for only one year out of seven would be grossly insufficient to rejuvenate the soil. Hopkins summarises as follows:

> Based on literary sources and on the practices of contemporary traditional farming communities, it appears that the sabbatical year law does not describe or enjoin a comprehensive or inclusive system of agricultural fallowing, though it does concretize and sanctify a single element of the whole. Present scholarship on the sabbatical-year law fails to see this distinction.[158]

In this respect, the sabbatarian fallow year forms only *part* of an agricultural practice of leaving land fallow for rejuvenation of the soil. However, it is this part of the agricultural practice which carried a special symbolic meaning and was therefore compulsory for all farmers, regardless of whatever other personal practice of leaving land fallow by alternation they pursued.

Hopkins highlights yet another benefit of the sabbath year in compelling a rehearsal for crop calamity. He states:

> Having seen the potential fit of a general year of fallowing into the cereal rotation, now imagine the demands that preparing for this year would make upon Highland agricultural systems. Mobilization of labor to increase pre-sabbatical year plowing and planting and to gather a larger harvest, construction of storage facilities, maintenance of distribution networks, and planning and coordination of community-wide efforts are all activities that such an institution would elicit. The practice of a general fallow year is no less than a simulation of a crisis of crop failure. It creates, tests, and maintains necessary devices for coping with such a failure – the consequences of which all adult members of a farming village would no doubt have vividly implanted in their memories. Besides satisfying any number of other community goals (e.g., it can also be interpreted as a social leveling device), the sabbatical-year law embodies a divinely sanctioned institution which would enforce

---

158. Hopkins, 194-95.

elasticity of agricultural production and promote social cohesion, both essentials for subsistence security.[159]

The sabbath year and the 'dropping' of debts

Some 38 years after the law was given, just before the Israelites were to enter the promised land, Moses in Deuteronomy 15:1-11 added a new dimension to the sabbath year. At the Feast of Booths in that year (Deut. 31:10) a 'dropping' of debts was to be proclaimed. The word used for this 'dropping' is formed from the word used in Exodus 23 to have the land 'lie fallow' in the seventh year.[160] It is self-evident that those who were in debt would be less likely to be able to pay their debt in a year when no harvest was forthcoming. For this reason debts were not to be collected during the sabbath year. Such debts were not cancelled, but postponed.

The penalty for non-observance

There are no civil penalties imposed for disregard of the law of the sabbath year. However, Leviticus 26:34-35 (cf. 2 Chron. 36:21) does warn that non observance will eventually be punished by exile for the number of years which the sabbath year is not observed by the nation. As it turns out, Israel did not observe this commandment and for this reason the nation served 70 years in exile. The covenant of those who had returned from exile made under the governor Nehemiah in 445 BC contained the stipulation that the sabbath year would be observed (Neh. 10:31b). Historical sources demonstrate that indeed the post-exilic community continued to observe the sabbath year for centuries thereafter.[161]

---

159. Hopkins, 273.
160. The verb is שמט 'to let loose', 'let drop'. Exodus 23:11 commands that the land 'be let loose', in other words left alone and not harvested. Deuteronomy 15:1 introduces a law of 'letting loose' (שְׁמִטָּה) in relation to debts.
161. See Jos. *Ant.* 11.343 (time of Alexander the Great); 1 Macc. 6:49, 53 (cf. Jos. *Ant.* 12.378, time of the Maccabean revolt); Jos. *Ant.* 13.234 (cf. *BJ* 1.60, 135-34 BC); *Ant.* 14.202 (44 BC); *Ant.* 475 (*ca.* 38-37 BC).

Text

¹⁰ Ἓξ ἔτη σπερεῖς τὴν γῆν σου καὶ συνάξεις τὰ γενήματα αὐτῆς· ¹¹ τῷ δὲ ἑβδόμῳ ἄφεσιν ποιήσεις καὶ ἀνήσεις αὐτήν, καὶ ἔδονται οἱ πτωχοὶ τοῦ ἔθνους σου, τὰ δὲ ὑπολειπόμενα ἔδεται τὰ θηρία τὰ ἄγρια. οὕτως ποιήσεις τὸν ἀμπελῶνά σου καὶ τὸν ἐλαιῶνά σου.	וְשֵׁשׁ שָׁנִים תִּזְרַע אֶת־אַרְצֶךָ וְאָסַפְתָּ אֶת־תְּבוּאָתָהּ: ¹¹ וְהַשְּׁבִיעִת תִּשְׁמְטֶנָּה וּנְטַשְׁתָּהּ וְאָכְלוּ אֶבְיֹנֵי עַמֶּךָ וְיִתְרָם תֹּאכַל חַיַּת הַשָּׂדֶה כֵּן־תַּעֲשֶׂה לְכַרְמְךָ לְזֵיתֶךָ:

שמט, *Qal* to let loose, let fall	יֶתֶר, rest, remainder
נטש, *Qal* leave fallow, uncultivated	

23:10

וְשֵׁשׁ שָׁנִים / Ἓξ ἔτη

The LXX shows no awareness of the copulative *waw*. Indeed the *waw* makes little sense, given that it would turn v.10 into a circumstantial clause and connect it – most improbably – to v.9. Note that שָׁנִים, despite the ending, is a feminine noun, hence שֵׁשׁ and not שִׁשָּׁה (cardinal numbers from 3-10 take the opposite gender to their related noun).

23:11

וְיִתְרָם / τὰ δὲ ὑπολειπόμενα

The LXX may deliberately not have translated the suffix, if present in the *Vorlage*. Note the omission of אֶת־, which is common when the direct object precedes the verb.

חַיַּת הַשָּׂדֶה / τὰ θηρία τὰ ἄγρια

While the adjective ἄγριος does literally mean 'of the field', the connotation in Greek is the opposite to the Hebrew. The phrase 'of the field' in Hebrew implies 'domestic' (i.e. belonging to the farm), while in Greek ἄγριος implies 'wild' or even 'savage'.

לְכַרְמְךָ לְזֵיתֶךָ / τὸν ἀμπελῶνά σου καὶ τὸν ἐλαιῶνά σου

The copulative in the text of both the LXX and Sam. Pent. is surely correct.

23:12

Six days work, one day rest (for animals, slaves, sojourners)

Translation

¹² Six days you may do your work, but on the seventh day you shall rest in order that your head of cattle and your donkey may rest and that your married-slave woman's son and the sojourner may be refreshed.

Commentary

Only one aspect of the sabbath day is mentioned here in this law, namely, that of ensuring that the work-animals (cattle, presumably oxen, and donkeys) and workers (male children of maid-servants) and sojourners (i.e. refugees) are provided the opportunity to rest on the sabbath day.[162] The fourth commandment in the law is invariably addressed to the heads of households. It is their responsibility to ensure that the household is provided with sabbath rest. It is for this reason that this law has no civil penalties. A slave is not punished for working on the sabbath since he has no choice. Free persons who work on the sabbath day are liable to the death penalty, but that aspect is not addressed in this law (cf. Exod. 31:12-17).

We may note that the sabbath law was a known entity. This is not only clear from the fact that the Israelites were already observing the sabbath before reaching Mount Sinai (cf. the gathering of manna in Exod. 16:21-30), but also from the wording. The verb enjoining

---

162. In Leviticus 23:3 a different aspect of the weekly sabbath day is mentioned, namely, the fact that it requires "a holy assembly" and is to be celebrated "in all your dwelling places", probably referring to all the villages, towns or cities.

that the married-slave woman's son and the sojourner 'be refreshed' (נפשׁ *Niph.*) is repeated at Exodus 31:17, where Yhwh is said to have been 'refreshed' on the seventh day after having created the heaven and earth in the previous six days. The verb is only ever used three times in all of the Old Testament, which highlights the connection made between God's refreshing after creation and the refreshing of the weekly sabbath.

It is interesting to note the difference between the law of the sabbath year, which is not directly penalised, and the law of the weekly sabbath, which incurs the death penalty for free persons who choose to work. This sets the weekly sabbath off as a distinct moral entity from the symbolism of the sabbath year.

Text

¹² ἓξ ἡμέρας ποιήσεις τὰ ἔργα σου, τῇ δὲ ἡμέρᾳ τῇ ἑβδόμῃ ἀναπαύσῃ, ἵνα ἀναπαύσηται ὁ βοῦς σου καὶ τὸ ὑποζύγιόν σου, καὶ ἵνα ἀναψύξῃ ὁ υἱὸς τῆς παιδίσκης σου καὶ ὁ προσήλυτος.	שֵׁשֶׁת יָמִים תַּעֲשֶׂה מַעֲשֶׂיךָ וּבַיּוֹם הַשְּׁבִיעִי תִּשְׁבֹּת לְמַעַן יָנוּחַ שׁוֹרְךָ וַחֲמֹרֶךָ וְיִנָּפֵשׁ בֶּן־אֲמָתְךָ וְהַגֵּר׃

נפשׁ, *Niph.* to breathe freely, recover (used only 3x)

23:12

תַּעֲשֶׂה מַעֲשֶׂיךָ

> Note the omission of אֶת־, which is not always readily explainable, although if it is lacking with a direct object placed after its verb, there are generally no words intervening between verb and object.

וַחֲמֹרֶךָ

> Note the pausal form before a new clause (regularly: וַחֲמֹרֶךָ).

23:13

No mention of other gods

Translation

¹³ You shall be on your guard in respect of all which I have said to you, but the names of other gods you shall not make known. They shall not be heard upon your lips.[163]

Commentary

This law reminds the Israelites that they are to carefully heed what Y<small>HWH</small> has spoken to them and in connection with that to be sure not to 'mention' the names of other gods. But we may ask what the practical import of not 'mentioning' other gods is. The verb used (זכר *Hiph.*) literally refers to 'causing remembrance', but it is used in the sense of 'mentioning' or 'making known'. In Psalm 16:4 David promises not to take up the names of other gods upon his lips in the context of pagan worship (drink offerings of blood), but the terminology is quite different to Exodus 23 and there is no direct connection to this law. Closer in wording is what God says in Hosea 2:16-17 (Hebr. vs.18-19), namely, that he will remove the names of the Baals from Israel's mouth and they will no longer 'be remembered' (זכר *Niph.*) by their name (similarly Zech. 13:2). Perhaps the best indication is what Joshua says in Joshua 23:7b where the same prohibition is given as follows: "and you shall neither mention *nor swear* by the name of their gods". These parallels suggest that the intent of the law is more than just prohibiting the worship of other gods. In fact, that is in all probability not the main point at all. If the worship of Y<small>HWH</small> alone is assumed, then this law is forbidding naming other gods when contracts or covenants are sealed. This may effectively prohibit covenants with non-Israelites, given that

---

163. Lit. "(the name of other gods) shall not be heard upon your mouth".

in such contractual oaths the parties could be expected to swear both by their own god(s) and the god(s) of the other party.

Text

¹³ πάντα, ὅσα εἴρηκα πρὸς ὑμᾶς, φυλάξασθε. καὶ ὄνομα θεῶν ἑτέρων οὐκ ἀναμνησθήσεσθε, οὐδὲ μὴ ἀκουσθῇ ἐκ τοῦ στόματος ὑμῶν.	וּבְכֹל אֲשֶׁר־אָמַרְתִּי אֲלֵיכֶם תִּשָּׁמֵרוּ וְשֵׁם אֱלֹהִים אֲחֵרִים לֹא תַזְכִּירוּ לֹא יִשָּׁמַע עַל־פִּיךָ׃

23:13

וּבְכֹל ... תִּשָּׁמֵרוּ / πάντα ... φυλάξασθε

The *Niph.* שמר, even when used reflexively, does not take a direct object: "you shall be on your guard concerning/in all …". Once again the LXX is surely correct in omitting the initial copulative (see the comment at 23:10).

עַל־פִּיךָ / ἐκ τοῦ στόματος ὑμῶν

The singular pronominal suffix in MT is unexpected and incongruent. The Sam.Pent. offers an alternate solution to the LXX, namely, retaining the singular suffix and reading the verb תַזְכִּירוּ as the singular תַזְכִּיר, attaching the *waw* to the following לֹא as a conjunction. This only shifts the problem, given that the Sam.Pent. still retains the plural verb in the initial clause.

23:14-17

Three annual feasts

Translation

¹⁴ Three times in the year you will celebrate a feast to me.

¹⁵ You will keep the feast of unleavened bread. Seven days you will eat unleavened bread just as I commanded you at the assembly of the month of grain-ears (Abib) for in that month you went out from Egypt. And my face will not be seen with empty hands.

¹⁶ And (you will keep) the feast of the grain harvest, the first-fruits of your labour, which you sow in the field and the harvest of the ingathering at the end of the year when you gather (the fruit of) your labour from the field.

¹⁷ Three times in the year every one of your males will see the face of the Lord, YHWH.

Commentary

The three compulsory feasts to YHWH are now briefly outlined. The commandment for all the males to appear is repeated several times in the law (Exod. 23:17; 34:23-24; Deut. 16:16, cf. 2 Chron. 8:13). The census at the time of the law counted adult males from the age of twenty and upwards. We may presume, in accordance with later tradition (cf. Jub. 49:17), that all males twenty and older were expected to attend the feasts. The wording of these commands is that the males 'see the face of the Lord, YHWH', which is an expression for appearing in his temple.[164] This requirement, however, does not

---

164. Given that this way of expressing the matter is common in the law, the text of 23:15 and 17 is usually emended to conform (as they stand, they make no grammatical sense). For details, see the textual commentary.

prevent women, children, slaves or sojourners from attending the feasts (cf. 1 Sam. 1:3-4). Such attendance in Jerusalem of at least all the adult male citizens simultaneously three times a year does involve taking definite risks, given that properties all over Israel would be left quite vulnerable to attack and plundering. For this reason God adds in Exodus 34:24 that he will personally provide protection at these times. Attendance at the feasts is a demonstration of trust in God.

The first feast in the calendar is that in 'the month of Abib' (lit. 'the month of the ears of grain'), that is, March / April. Passover is not mentioned, only the ensuing seven day festival of unleavened bread, which is directly tied to the exodus from Egypt. It is possible that Passover is understood to be subsumed in this feast.[165]

A final clause commanding those attending the feast not to come empty-handed is added. In Deuteronomy 16:16 this clause (which appears several times in the law) applies to all three feasts. It is probably mentioned here, given that the other two feasts by their nature as harvest feasts require one to bring specific offerings. Here, the law emphasises that even at the feast of unleavened bread one ought to bring gifts to God.

The second feast in the calendar is the feast of ingathering of grain (*qātsīr*), further defined as the first-fruits of what has been sown. This feast, otherwise known as 'Pentecost', is celebrated for one day.

The third feast is that of the (grain) harvest (*'āsīr*) towards the end of the year, a feast lasting eight days.[166]

---

165. The wording of v.15 is virtually identical to that in 34:18, excepting the final clause which is found in 34:20c.
166. For a more detailed discussion of these three feasts see Anderson[5].

Text

¹⁴ Τρεῖς καιροὺς τοῦ ἐνιαυτοῦ ἑορτάσατέ μοι. ¹⁵ τὴν ἑορτὴν τῶν ἀζύμων φυλάξασθε ποιεῖν· ἑπτὰ ἡμέρας ἔδεσθε ἄζυμα, καθάπερ ἐνετειλάμην σοι, κατὰ τὸν καιρὸν τοῦ μηνὸς τῶν νέων· ἐν γὰρ αὐτῷ ἐξῆλθες ἐξ Αἰγύπτου. οὐκ ὀφθήσῃ ἐνώπιόν μου κενός. ¹⁶ καὶ ἑορτὴν θερισμοῦ πρωτογενημάτων ποιήσεις τῶν ἔργων σου, ὧν ἂν σπείρῃς ἐν τῷ ἀγρῷ σου, καὶ ἑορτὴν συντελείας ἐπ' ἐξόδου τοῦ ἐνιαυτοῦ ἐν τῇ συναγωγῇ τῶν ἔργων σου τῶν ἐκ τοῦ ἀγροῦ σου. ¹⁷ τρεῖς καιροὺς τοῦ ἐνιαυτοῦ ὀφθήσεται πᾶν ἀρσενικόν σου ἐνώπιον κυρίου τοῦ θεοῦ σου.

¹⁵ שָׁלֹשׁ רְגָלִים תָּחֹג לִי בַּשָּׁנָה: אֶת־חַג הַמַּצּוֹת תִּשְׁמֹר שִׁבְעַת יָמִים תֹּאכַל מַצּוֹת כַּאֲשֶׁר צִוִּיתִךָ לְמוֹעֵד חֹדֶשׁ הָאָבִיב כִּי־בוֹ יָצָאתָ מִמִּצְרָיִם וְלֹא־יֵרָאוּ פָנַי רֵיקָם: ¹⁶ וְחַג הַקָּצִיר בִּכּוּרֵי מַעֲשֶׂיךָ אֲשֶׁר תִּזְרַע בַּשָּׂדֶה וְחַג הָאָסִף בְּצֵאת הַשָּׁנָה בְּאָסְפְּךָ אֶת־מַעֲשֶׂיךָ מִן־הַשָּׂדֶה: ¹⁷ שָׁלֹשׁ פְּעָמִים בַּשָּׁנָה יֵרָאֶה כָּל־זְכוּרְךָ אֶל־פְּנֵי הָאָדֹן יְהוָה:

חֹדֶשׁ, new moon, month	רֵיקָם (with adverbial ending -*am*) with empty hands
מוֹעֵד, place for meeting; meeting, assembly; appointed time	קָצִיר, grain cutting (i.e. grain harvest)
אָבִיב, ears of grain (already ripe, but still soft, to be eaten either crushed or roasted)	אָסִף, harvest (only used twice, here and Exod. 34:22)

23:14

שָׁלֹשׁ רְגָלִים / τρεῖς καιροὺς τοῦ ἐνιαυτοῦ

This expression is used four times in the Old Testament, where the plural 'feet' means 'times'. Each occurrence is also together with the number '3'. A more usual word would פַּעַם (cf. v.17). See Jouön/Muraoka §142q. The LXX has either read שָׁלֹשׁ פְּעָמִים בַּשָּׁנָה or deducted from v.17a that this must be the intended meaning. Note that both רְגָלִים and פְּעָמִים (v.17), despite their endings, are feminine nouns, hence שָׁלֹשׁ and not שְׁלֹשָׁה (cardinal numbers from 3-10 take the opposite gender to their related noun).

תָּחֹג / ἑορτάσατε

As is more common, the LXX uses the imperative for an imperfect giving a command. More unusual is that the LXX places the first three verbs of this law (ἑορτάσατε, φυλάξασθε, ἔδεσθε) in the plural before resorting to the singular.

23:15

תֹּאכַל ... תִּשְׁמֹר / φυλάξασθε ποιεῖν ... ἔδεσθε
The LXX possibly read: תִּשְׁמְרוּ לַעֲשׂוֹת ... תֹּאכְלוּ.

וְלֹא־יֵרָאוּ פָנַי / οὐκ ὀφθήσῃ ἐνώπιόν μου

The LXX lacks the copulative. The idea of worshippers coming to the temple and seeing God's face (ראה את פני יהוה) is quite common in the Old Testament. For this reason most scholars presume that the several phrases such as this one where the verb is pointed *Niphal* are a secondary alteration (already present in the LXX) of an original *Qal* out of respect for Exod. 33:20 ("you cannot see my face, for man shall not see me and live."). Therefore even texts such as Exod. 34:23 are pointed *Niph.* despite the definite object marker (which with the *Niphal* is probably to be taken as אֵת = 'with'): יֵרָאֶה כָּל־זְכוּרְךָ אֶת־פְּנֵי הָאָדֹן. We should therefore probably read: וְלֹא־יִרְאוּ פָנַי, lit. "and they will not see my face …" although here the plural should be taken as the impersonal third person plural substituting for a passive, given the second person singular suffixes in the foregoing. In this verse, of course, reading the verb as *Niphal* makes no difference given that the (plural) noun 'face' would then be the subject.

23:16

וְחַג הַקָּצִיר בִּכּוּרֵי מַעֲשֶׂיךָ / καὶ ἑορτὴν θερισμοῦ πρωτογενημάτων ποιήσεις τῶν ἔργων σου

One might suppose the LXX to have read: וְחַג קָצִיר בִּכּוּרִים תַּעֲשֶׂה מִמַּעֲשֶׂיךָ, however we would then surely have expected ἀπὸ τῶν ἔργων. This may suggest that the LXX has added a verb for the sense. MT depends upon the main verb of v.15. Nevertheless the LXX may have correctly read קָצִיר.

בַּשָּׂדֶה / ἐν τῷ ἀγρῷ σου ... מִן־הַשָּׂדֶה / ἐκ τοῦ ἀγροῦ σου
The LXX reads the 2nd pers. sing. suffix (שָׂדְךָ) twice in this verse.

23:17

יֵרָאֶה כָּל־זְכוּרְךָ אֶל־פְּנֵי הָאָדֹן יְהוָה / ὀφθήσεται πᾶν ἀρσενικόν σου ἐνώπιον κυρίου τοῦ θεοῦ σου

See the note at v.15 and particularly the quotation from Exod. 34:23. It is clear that אֶל should be emended to אֶת (the marker אֶת־ is also the reading of the Sam. Pent.) and that we should point *Qal* instead of *Niphal*. The expression הָאָדֹן יְהוָה is only used here and Exod. 34:32 (the Sam. Pent. omits the definite article). The LXX presupposes יהוה אֱלֹהֶיךָ. The noun זכור is used as a collective of זָכָר ('male').

23:18

Don't offer blood with leaven nor leave fat until morning

Translation

¹⁸ You shall not sacrifice the blood of my sacrifice with leavened bread and the fat of my feast shall not remain overnight until morning.

Commentary

The sacrifice

Sacrifices were generally a mixture of items tied upon an altar and set alight. A regular set of sacrifices included an animal for a whole burnt offering, a grain offering, the fat and kidneys of the animal used for a peace offering as well as a libation of wine and a sprinkling of salt. The blood of the animals to be used was splashed against the foot of the altar. This was done before the animals were even skinned and cut up to prepare the sacrifice. As such the blood ritual, which signified atonement (Lev. 17:10-12), was separated from the actual sacrifice. Strictly speaking, blood would never combine with leaven on an altar. However, we need not be so pedantic. The point of the first part of this law is that the bread-cakes used for a grain offering that is offered on the altar – against which the blood has been splashed – may not contain leaven (cf. Lev. 2:11-12; Exod. 34:25).[167] The sacrifice itself represented God's meal (cf. Lev. 3:11; Ps. 50). God's portions, piled

---

167. Loaves of bread with leaven were used as wave offerings at Pentecost (Lev. 23:17) and viewed as first-fruits. The peace offering for thanksgiving (with its accompanying grain offerings of unleavened bread) were provided with leavened loaves of bread for the use of the priest (Lev. 7:13-14; Am. 4:5).

up and tied upon the altar (his food-table), were burned to convert them into a sweet-smelling aroma which ascended to him and in which he took pleasure. The bread portion allotted to God for his symbolic meal was to be unleavened. For this reason, the portions of God's meal which were not burned, but reserved for his servants, the priests, were also unleavened (Lev. 6:14-18 = Hebr. 6:7-11). Only the bread prepared for the meal of those bringing the sacrifices was permitted to be leavened. This was the bread that went with the people's portion of the peace offerings. Although the first animal (the whole-burnt offering) was given entirely to God, the second animal (the peace offering) was available for eating by those bringing the sacrifice, after the best portions of it, namely the fat and kidneys, had been removed for God. The Passover sacrifice was the only exception to this. The Passover lamb was essentially a special kind of peace offering where the bread had to remain unleavened and the meat was to be roasted instead of boiled.

Leaven

Leaven was old dough which had become sour and thus appropriate material for fermentation. The feast of *unleavened* bread connected with the Passover had a special reason for banning leaven. It was a memorial to the fact that the Israelites had left Egypt in such a hurry that there had been no time to prepare leavened bread (Exod. 12:33-39; Deut. 16:1-8). This fact, however, did not explain why God's meals presented on his altar banned leaven. Although no explanation for this is given in the Old Testament, Jewish tradition attributed the ban on leaven to the fact that its 'rotting' fermentation was symbolic of sin. It is this traditional Jewish explanation for the prohibition of leaven with sacrifices that is echoed by the apostle Paul in 1 Corinthians 5:6-8. There he contrasts "the leaven of malice and evil" with "the unleavened bread of sincerity and truth". For Paul, as for Jews generally, this explanation was also used with respect to the unleavened bread eaten together with the Passover lamb.

Fat

The fat of any kind of animal appropriate for sacrifice was considered to be the choicest part and therefore reserved for God.[168] No Israelite was to eat it upon pain of immediate 'cutting off' (cf. Lev. 7:23-25). The fat (and therefore the sacrifice as a whole) was to be offered up on the same day that the animal was slain. The word 'fat' was often used more generally for those cuts of the peace offering (fat, kidneys) which were to be placed with the burnt offering on the altar (e.g. Lev. 9:24; Isa. 1:11, cf. 1 Sam. 15:22; 1 Kgs 8:64) and that is probably the meaning here. Elsewhere the prohibition of leaving sacrificial meat over until the morning is specifically applied to that meat of the peace offering, which was to be eaten by the offerer (Lev. 7:15; Exod. 34:25; Deut. 16:4). Exodus 34:25 and Deuteronomy 16:4 apply specifically to the Passover peace offering and both those prohibitions also follow directly upon a rule forbidding leaven.[169] Here, however, it is the *fat*, that is, God's portion, which is not to be left until morning. This may suggest that there was a temptation to set aside some of the fat of the sacrifice so that it could be used the following morning on the altar, perhaps in order to accompany the utilisation of some leftover meat to be eaten by the offerer.

Text

[18] ὅταν γὰρ ἐκβάλω ἔθνη ἀπὸ προσώπου σου, καὶ ἐμπλατύνω τὰ ὅριά σου, οὐ θύσεις ἐπὶ ζύμῃ αἷμα θυσιάσματός μου, οὐδὲ μὴ κοιμηθῇ στέαρ τῆς ἑορτῆς μου ἕως πρωί,	לֹא־תִזְבַּח עַל־חָמֵץ דַּם־זִבְחִי וְלֹא־יָלִין חֵלֶב־חַגִּי עַד־בֹּקֶר:

---

168. For this reason the word 'fat' in Hebrew is also used metaphorically for 'the choicest / best'. That it was considered God's food is clear from Lev. 3:14-16; Isa. 1:11; 43:24; Ezek. 44:7 cf. Deut. 32:37-38.

169. For this reason Jewish tradition connects both the laws in this verse with the feast of Passover. There is, however, no justification for this in the context.

| חָמֵץ, leavened (food) (cf. חמץ, Qal to be leavened) ל'ין, Qal to stay overnight | θῠσίασμα, ατος, τό, = θυσία (only used in the LXX) |

23:18

ὅταν γὰρ ἐκβάλω ἔθνη ἀπὸ προσώπου σου καὶ ἐμπλατύνω τὰ ὅριά σου

The LXX seems to have taken the first phrase from Exod. 34:24: כִּי־אוֹרִישׁ גּוֹיִם מִפָּנֶיךָ וְהִרְחַבְתִּי אֶת־גְּבוּלֶךָ.

עַל־חָמֵץ

The preposition עַל ('on') can also carry the nuance 'together with' or 'in addition to'.

דַּם־זִבְחִי / αἷμα θυσιάσματός μου

Note the lack of the definite direct object marker, which is less common when the direct object does not immediately follow the verb. This must also have been lacking in the text before the LXX translator, although this should not make דַּם indefinite as the translator seemed to think.

23:19a

First-fruits to be brought

Translation

¹⁹ᵃ You shall bring the best of the first-fruits of your ground into the house of Yhwh your God.

Commentary

The law of the first-fruits has been discussed above at the exposition of 22:29.

Text

| ¹⁹ᵃ τὰς ἀπαρχὰς τῶν πρωτογενημάτων τῆς γῆς σου εἰσοίσεις εἰς τὸν οἶκον κυρίου τοῦ θεοῦ σου. | רֵאשִׁית בִּכּוּרֵי אַדְמָתְךָ תָּבִיא בֵּית יְהוָה אֱלֹהֶיךָ |

23:19a

רֵאשִׁית בִּכּוּרֵי אַדְמָתְךָ

Note the omission of אֶת־, which is common when the direct object precedes the verb.

בֵּית יְהוָה / εἰς τὸν οἶκον κυρίου

We should probably read with the LXX בְּבֵית יהוה or with the Sam. Pent. בֵּיתָה יהוה.

23:19b

Don't boil a kid in its mother's milk

Translation

¹⁹ᵇ You shall not boil a kid in the milk of its mother.

Commentary

The following requirement (repeated in Exod. 34:26 and Deut. 14:21) that a kid not be boiled in its mother's milk has engendered much debate. It functions as the basis of the orthodox Jewish separation of milk and meat in the kitchen, a tradition going back at least to the Mishnah (third century AD).[170] It is, however, highly unlikely that this is the intention of the law. Even Abraham had combined milk products and meat in the meal he prepared for visiting angels (Gen. 18:8). Indeed this law is much more specific than a general requirement to separate milk and meat products. Since the time of Maimonides (12ᵗʰ cent. AD) certain interpreters have suggested that the law must have its background in some pagan ritual. The problem is that no pagan ritual is known involving boiling a kid in its mother's milk.

It ought to be noted that boiling meat was the most common method of preparation (cf. Judg 6:19). In fact, apart from the Passover Lamb, all sacrificial meat was to be boiled. We are not told what the meat was boiled in, but this law would suggest that it was quite common to

---

170. The tradition may, in fact, go back to the first century. According to the Mishnah, at least some aspects of the separation of milk and meat products seem to have been debated between the schools of Hillel and Shammai, cf. Mishnah, *Hullin* 8.1. There is, however, no other evidence indicating that this tradition was known at that time.

boil meat in milk. This had the advantage that unpleasant odours and flavours were significantly diminished.[171]

What this law is then saying is that a kid (*g^ethī* / גְּדִי, that is the young of either sheep or goat), if it is to be boiled in milk, must not be boiled in the milk of its mother. Given that there is nothing unsanitary or ritually unclean in doing this, we must conclude that the law is concerned about protecting the parent-child relationship. We may compare the laws against slaughtering cattle on the same day as their young and capturing a mother bird along with her fledglings or her eggs, and also the requirement that newborn cattle remain with their mothers at least a week before they may be sacrificed (cf. Exod. 22:30; Lev. 22:27–28; Deut. 22:6–7). This interpretation was also embraced by the Alexandrian Jewish commentator Philo around the beginning of the first century AD (*de virtut.* 142-44).

Text

[19b] οὐχ ἑψήσεις ἄρνα ἐν γάλακτι μητρὸς αὐτοῦ.	לֹא־תְבַשֵּׁל גְּדִי בַּחֲלֵב אִמּוֹ׃

בשׁל, *Piel* to make to be boiled

---

171   The Israelites also used water, cf. Exod. 12:9.

Appendices

The Effect of the Sin of the Golden Calf

In the following pages some of the more salient points relating to the effect of the sin of the golden calf for the regulations given by God to Israel are sketched.

When Israel arrived at Mt. Sinai God told them that they were to be "a kingdom of priests and a holy nation" (Exod. 19:6). Every family could send a priest to serve the Lord in his sanctuary according to what God had said at the exodus and indicated by the Passover feast, namely, that he would claim every first-born son for Himself. We read in Exodus 13:2

> Consecrate to me all the firstborn. Whatever is the first to open the womb among the people of Israel, both of man and of beast, is mine.

The beasts would be sacrificed to God. The first-born sons would be dedicated to God's service in his sanctuary. Indeed, already in the book of Genesis we see that God laid claim to first-born sons in the story of the sacrifice of Isaac (cf. Abel sacrificing the first-born of his flock, Gen. 4:4). And so it is that in the Book of the Covenant (which precedes the sin with the golden calf) the provision for redemption of first-born sons is not even mentioned:

> You shall not delay your harvest or your juice. The first-born of your sons you shall give to me. Thus you shall do for your cattle and for your flock, it will remain seven days with its mother, on the eighth day you will give it to me. (Exod. 22:29-30, my translation)[172]

---

172. See further the main commentary on Exod. 22:29-30. Note that Exod. 13:11-16 gives the law as it applied in the promised land. Given that it speaks of the redemption of first-born sons, the law clarifies to the reader (presumed to

From what we have adduced it is reasonable to conclude that the 'priests' who served under the Israelites when they arrived at Mt. Sinai were first-born sons (see Exod. 19:22-24).[173]

All this was to change after the Israelites profaned themselves by worshipping God in the form of a golden calf.[174] The law *after* this incident provides for redemption:

> *All that open the womb are mine, all your male livestock, the firstborn of cow and sheep. The firstborn of a donkey you shall redeem with a lamb, or if you will not redeem it you shall break its neck. All the firstborn of your sons you shall redeem. And none shall appear before me empty-handed.* (Exod. 34:19-20)

In fact, after the sin with the golden calf this redemption became mandatory for that Israelite generation.[175] The tabernacle was no longer to be staffed by first-born sons, but instead of the service of the first-born sons the Levites were appointed. We read in Numbers 3:12-13 ...

> *Behold, I have taken the Levites from among the people of Israel instead of every firstborn who opens the womb among the people of Israel. The Levites shall be mine, for all the firstborn are mine. On the day that I struck down all the firstborn in the land of Egypt, I consecrated for my own all the firstborn in Israel, both of man and of beast. They shall be mine: I am the* LORD.

In the same chapter we read that both the first-born sons of the Israelites and the Levites were counted off, but it was found that there were

---

be in the promised land) what the law means for him now. The transition from first-born sons dedicated to God to first-born sons being redeemed only actually occurred at Mt. Sinai (see below).
173. The law of Exod. 20:24-26 presupposes that a pre-Aaronic priest would be wearing some kind of simple linen loincloth which upon the ascent of stairs would expose one's genitals (cf. 2 Sam. 6:14, 20).
174. That Aaron intended the golden calf to be a representation of Y$_{HWH}$ is clear from Exod. 32:5. This was ultimately sin against the second commandment, not the first.
175. Later, because of the continuing service of the Levites, redemption was also the rule, although first-born sons seem to occasionally have been given to the temple as the case of the prophet Samuel suggests (1 Sam. 1).

273 more first-born sons than there were Levites. These 273 sons had therefore to pay a ransom of five shekels per person to redeem them from the temple service.[176] And henceforth the Lord expected that five shekels be paid to redeem every first born son (Num. 18:15-16).

Why did the Levites replace the first-born among the Israelites? When Moses returned from the mountain and discovered the great sin of the Israelites, Scripture records:

> *then Moses stood in the gate of the camp and said, "Who is on the LORD's side? Come to me." And all the sons of Levi gathered around him. And he said to them, "Thus says the LORD God of Israel, 'Put your sword on your side each of you, and go to and fro from gate to gate throughout the camp, and each of you kill his brother and his companion and his neighbor.'" And the sons of Levi did according to the word of Moses. And that day about three thousand men of the people fell.* (Exod. 32:26-28)

The Lord Jesus would later reflect on this incident when he warned his disciples:

> *For I have come to set a man against his father, and a daughter against her mother, and a daughter-in-law against her mother-in-law. And a person's enemies will be those of his own household. Whoever loves father or mother more than me is not worthy of me, and whoever loves son or daughter more than me is not worthy of me. And whoever does not take his cross and follow me is not worthy of me. Whoever finds his life will lose it, and whoever loses his life for my sake will find it.* (Matt. 10:35-39)

Because of the fact that the Levites showed such great dedication to YHWH that they were even willing to meteced out his drastic punishment

---

[176]. We also read that the cattle of the Levites was taken in the place of the (already mature) first-born among the cattle of the Israelites. This was evidently a ruling which prevented much of the cattle born to the Israelite herds in the preceding years from being confiscated. Henceforth the newly born first offspring would need to be dedicated to the Lord. No similar provision is recorded with respect to the flocks or to the donkeys, but a similar rule was probably applied.

in this fashion, they were chosen to serve him. Deuteronomy 33:8-11 records it as follows:

> *And of Levi he* (i.e. Moses) *said, "Give to Levi your Thummim, and your Urim to your godly one, whom you tested at Massah, with whom you quarreled at the waters of Meribah; who said of his father and mother, I regard them not'; he disowned his brothers and ignored his children. For they observed your word and kept your covenant. They shall teach Jacob your rules and Israel your law; they shall put incense before you and whole burnt offerings on your altar. Bless, O* LORD, *his substance, and accept the work of his hands; crush the loins of his adversaries, of those who hate him, that they rise not again."*

In this way the Levites reversed a curse which had long ago been placed upon their tribe because of the cruel action of the brothers Simeon and Levi to avenge the rape of their sister Dinah (Gen. 34). The patriarch Jacob had worded the curse as follows:

> *Simeon and Levi are brothers; weapons of violence are their swords. Let my soul come not into their council; O my glory, be not joined to their company. For in their anger they killed men, and in their willfulness they hamstrung oxen. Cursed be their anger, for it is fierce, and their wrath, for it is cruel! I will divide them in Jacob and scatter them in Israel.* (Gen. 49:5-7)

Because the tribe of Levi dedicated themselves to YHWH after the dreadful sin with the golden calf, he put a new twist on this curse. Yes, they would be scattered in Israel, but no longer as a sign of shame. They would be given special privileges, special cities, flocks and herds because they would be responsible for teaching the people God's laws and serving him in worship. Only the tribe of Simeon would remain scattered in shame.

It is this changed situation with respect to the personnel of the tabernacle which also explains why only first-fruits and not tithes are mentioned in the Book of the Covenant. If the original intent was to staff the tabernacle with first-born sons from Israelite families, these families would have been expected to see to it that their sons, who served the tabernacle, would be fed, housed and clothed. The income for the tabernacle was restricted to the first-fruits of crops and animals. The situation changed when Levites would be those staffing the tabernacle. Their tribe was not going to inherit any land. Therefore along with the change in personnel came a change in the income required for the tabernacle in order to see to it that the priests and Levites doing the service would be taken care of. This was provided by the law of the tithe (Num. 18:21-32). In Deuteronomy it is further stipulated that, in the third and sixth years of every seven year cycle, the tithes (after what has been used for the feasts) be deposited in the local towns and villages for the use of the local Levites, as well as sojourners, orphans and widows.[177]

We ought also to note that the coming of Jesus Christ, the only-begotten Son of God, to die for our sins has abolished the need to redeem first-born sons from serving God in formal public worship. The Levitical priesthood has been done away with and Christ is now the High-priest of the family of God's church. He is, as it were, the great first-born son among many brothers (cf. Rom. 8:29; Hebr. 2:11-12). We may also partake in his priesthood and offer ourselves up as thankofferings to God (Rom. 12:1). The original promise of Exodus 19:6 has in Christ found its final fulfilment (cf. 1Pet. 2:9; Rev. 1:6). Hebrews 12 depicts the New Testament church worshipping before the heavenly sanctuary as first-born priests (Hebr. 12:23).

---

177. On the interpretation of the tithe laws, see Anderson[12].

Finances in Hebrew

Money
Money is usually expressed with the commodity of silver:

כֶּסֶף, silver (τὸ ἀργύριον)[178]

Buying and Selling
In relation to buying we have the following terms:

קנה, *Qal.* to buy

מִקְנָה, acquisition, purchase

סֵפֶר מִקְנָה, document of sale

כֶּסֶף מִקְנָה, purchase price

קִנְיָן, property / possession

Less common (and not directly used of financial transactions) are ...

רכשׁ, *Qal.* to acquire (only used in Genesis)

רְכוּשׁ, what is acquired, possessions

עמר, *Hithp.* to trade (used twice in Deuteronomy of trading in people)

For selling we have the following terms:

מכר, *Qal.* to sell (ἀποδίδομαι, πωλέω)

מֶכֶר, purchase price (2x); saleable items (1x)

Lending and Borrowing
There are various verbs used of lending and borrowing. A quite morally neutral term is:

---

178. Greek also uses τὰ χρήματα for money (lit. 'things needed', cf. χράομαι)

לוֹה, *Qal.* to borrow (κίχραμαι)

    Hiph. to lend (i.e. 'cause to borrow') (κίχρημι)

Much less common (3x in Deuteronomy) and based on the noun עֲבוֹט (*deposit*) is:

    עבט, *Qal.* 1. to borrow; 2. to accept a deposit + acc.

    Hiph. to lend against a secured deposit

The interest on such a loan is expressed by:

    נֶשֶׁךְ, interest (ὁ τόκος, lit. 'offspring', cf. τίκτω)

Derived from that noun is a verb occasionally used:

    נשׁךְ, *Qal.* to lend on interest (used twice with the same meaning in the *Hiph.*).

Contractual lending, implying interest (often used in a negative sense) is:

    נשׁא / נשׁה, *Qal.* to lend out (at contractual interest) (with בְּ) (δανείζω)

    Hiph. to cheat, deceive + acc. or with לְ (cf. causing one to lend out money on false pretences)

Derived from this verb we have the following nouns:

    מַשָּׁא, interest, debt (a more contractual term than נֶשֶׁךְ)

    מַשָּׁאָה, contractual loan (τὸ δάνειον)

When a loan was contracted, often a pledge was taken. The corresponding terms are:

    חבל, *Qal.* to take a pledge (ἐνεχυράζω)

    חֲבֹל, pledge (ἡ ἐγγύη, lit. something put into the palm of the hand, cf. ἐγγυαλίζω)

One could also stand surety for a debtor:

    ערב, *Qal.* to stand surety for + acc. of debtor (ἐγγυάω, 'to give as a pledge', *Mid.* 'to pledge oneself' / 'give security')

From which we get several related words for 'pledge':

עֲרֻבָּה, pledge, security (ἡ ὑποθήκη, 'pledge' / 'deposit')

עֵרָבוֹן, pledge, security

Property

אֲחֻזָּה, property (esp. landed property) (cf. אחז 'to seize, grasp, hold on to')

נַחֲלָה, inalienable inherited property

הוֹן, wealth, property

Bibliography

ANDERSON[1], R. D., "A Law for Jealous Husbands: Num. 5:11-31". Available: http://anderson.genevanconsort.com/ancient-hebrew

ANDERSON[2], R. D., "De Doodstraf in Gods Wet". Available: http://anderson.genevanconsort.com/artikelen-en-preken

ANDERSON[3], R. D., "The Jealous Husband". Available: http://anderson.genevanconsort.comarticles

ANDERSON[4], R. D., "The Laws for Uncleanness in the Pentateuch and NT Baptism". Available: http://anderson.genevanconsort.com/articles

ANDERSON[5], R. D., "The Three Great Feasts in the Worship of Israel". Available: http://anderson.genevanconsort.com/articles

ANDERSON[6], R. D., "The Use of God's Law". Available: http://anderson.genevanconsort.com/articles

ANDERSON[7], R. D., "Old Covenant vs. New Testament: The Dynamics of Covenant Theology from בְּרִית to διαθήκη". Available: http://anderson.genevanconsort.com/articles

ANDERSON[8], R. D., "Ernst Jenni on the *Piel* in Hebrew". Available: http://anderson.genevanconsort.com/ancient-languages/ancient-hebrew

ANDERSON[9], R. D., "Greek Word Order in Contrast to Hebrew". Available: http://anderson.genevanconsort.com/ancient-languages/ancient-greek

ANDERSON[10], R. D., "Animal Story". Available: http://anderson.genevanconsort.com/ancient-languages/ancient-greek

ANDERSON[11], R. D., "The Question of the Temple Tax: A Reader". Available: http://anderson.genevanconsort.com/ancient-languages/ancient-greek

ANDERSON[12], R. D., "Tithe Law Interpretations". Available: http://anderson.genevanconsort.com/articles

BAUMANN, A., "זָלַל" in *Theological Dictionary of the Old Testament*, vol. 3, ed. G. J. Botterweck and H. Ringgren, transl. J. T. Willis *et al*, rev. ed. (Grand Rapids: Eerdmans, 1978).

CHILDS, B., *The Book of Exodus* (Philadelphia: Westminster Press, 1974).

CHIRICHIGNO, G. C., *Debt-Slavery in Israel and the Ancient Near East* (Sheffield: Academic Press, 1993).

CLINES, D. J. A. (ed.), *The Dictionary of Classical Hebrew*, 8 vols (Sheffield: Academic Press, 1993–2011).

DAVIDSON, A. B., *Introductory Hebrew Grammar*, 26th ed. rev. J. Mauchline (Edinburgh: T. & T. Clark, 1966).

DE VAUX, R., *Ancient Israel: Its Life and Institutions*, transl. J. McHugh, second ed., (London: Darton, Longman & Todd, 1965).

DURHAM, J. I., *Exodus* (Dallas: Word, 1998).

GERSTENBERGER, E. "פלל" in *Theological Dictionary of the Old Testament*, vol. 11, ed. G. J. Botterweck, H. Ringgren and H.-J. Fabry, transl. D. E. Green (Grand Rapids: Eerdmans, 1998) 567-77.

GOW, A. S. F. and D. L. Page, *The Greek Anthology: The Garland of Philip and Some Contemporary Epigrams*, 2 vols. (Cambridge: University Press, 1968)

HOPKINS, D. C., *The Highlands of Canaan: Agricultural Life in the Early Iron Age*, SWBAS, 3 (Sheffield: Almond Press, 1985).

HORSLEY, G. H. R. (ed.), *New Documents Illustrating Early Christianity*, vol. 2 (Macquarie University Ancient History Documentary Research Centre, 1982)

HOUTMAN, C., *Exodus Deel 3*, Commentaar op het Oude Testament (Kampen: J. H. Kok, 1996).

HYATT, J. P., *Exodus*, The New Century Bible Commentary (Grand Rapids: Eerdmans, 1971).

JENNI[1], E., "Das Wort 'ōlām im Alten Testament" in *Zeitschrift für die Alttestamentliche Wissenschaft*, Vol. 64 (1952), 197-248 and Vol. 65 (1953), 1–35.

JENNI[2], E., *Das hebräische Pi'el: Syntaktisch-semasiologische Untersuchung einer Verbalform im Alten Testament* (Zürich: EVZ, 1968).

JENNI[3], E., "שׂנא hassen" in *Theologisches Handwörterbuch zum Alten Testament*, Band II (München: Chr. Kaiser Verlag, 1976) 835-37.

JENNI[4], E., "Nif'al und Hitpa'el im Biblisch-Hebräischen" in *Studien zur Sprachwelt des Alten Testaments III* (Stuttgart: Kohlhammer, 2012) 131-303.

JOHNSON, B., "מִשְׁפָּט" in *Theological Dictionary of the Old Testament*, vol. 9, ed. G. J. Botterweck, H. Ringgren and H.-J. Fabry, transl. D. E. Green (Grand Rapids: Eerdmans, 1998).

JOUÖN, P. & T. Muraoka, *A Grammar of Biblical Hebrew* (Rome: Pontificio Istituto Biblico, 2006).

KAUTZSCH, E., *Gesenius Hebrew Grammar*, rev. transl. of 28th German ed. by A. E. Cowley (Oxford: Clarendon Press, 1985 [corrected ed.]).

KOEHLER, L. & W. Baumgartner *et al.*, *The Hebrew and Aramaic Lexicon of the Old Testament* (Leiden: E. J. Brill, 1994–2000).

RICHARDSON, M. E. J., *Hammurabi's Laws: Text, Translation and Glossary* (London: T. & T. Clark, 2000).

ROTH, M. T. (ed.) *The Assyrian Dictionary of the Oriental Institute of the University of Chicago*, 21 vols. (Chicago: Oriental Institute, 1970-2010).

SANDERSON, J. E., *An Exodus Scroll from Qumran: 4QpaleoExod*[m] (Atlanta: Scholars Press, 1986).

SARNA, N. M., *Exodus*, The JPS Torah Commentary (Philadelphia: Jewish Publication Society, 1991).

SPRINKLE, J. M., *The Book of the Covenant: A Literary Approach*, JSOT Supplement Series 174 (Sheffield: Academic Press, 1994).

STRACK, H. L. & P. Billerbeck, *Kommentar zum Neuen Testament aus Talmud und Midrasch*, 6 vols (München: C. H. Beck, 1926-1961).

THACKERAY, H. J., *A Grammar of the Old Testament in Greek* (Cambridge: University Press, 1909).

TOV, E., "Texual Harmonization in Exodus 1 – 24" in *A Journal of Biblical Textual Criticism*, vol.22 (2017) 1-16.

VAN DAM, C., Unpublished lecture notes taken in 1988 at the *Theological College of the Canadian Reformed Churches*.

VAN DER MERWE, C. & J. Naudé; J. Kroeze, *A Biblical Hebrew Reference Grammar*, electronic ed. (Oak Harbor: Logos Research Systems, 1997).

WALTKE, B. K. and M. O'Connor, *An Introduction to Biblical Hebrew Syntax* (Winona Lake, Indiana: Eisenbrauns, 1990).

WEVERS, W., *Notes on the Greek Text of Exodus* (Atlanta: Scholars Press, 1990).

www.ingramcontent.com/pod-product-compliance
Lightning Source LLC
Chambersburg PA
CBHW051430290426
44109CB00016B/1497